Cambridge Elements

Elements in International Relations
edited by
Jon C. W. Pevehouse
University of Wisconsin–Madison
Tanja A. Börzel
Freie Universität Berlin
Edward D. Mansfield
University of Pennsylvania

THE RISE OF AUTHORITARIAN MIDDLE-POWERS AND WHAT IT MEANS FOR WORLD POLITICS

Marie-Eve Desrosiers
University of Ottawa

Nic Cheeseman
University of Birmingham

CAMBRIDGE
UNIVERSITY PRESS

Shaftesbury Road, Cambridge CB2 8EA, United Kingdom

One Liberty Plaza, 20th Floor, New York, NY 10006, USA

477 Williamstown Road, Port Melbourne, VIC 3207, Australia

314–321, 3rd Floor, Plot 3, Splendor Forum, Jasola District Centre, New Delhi – 110025, India

Cambridge University Press is part of Cambridge University Press & Assessment, a department of the University of Cambridge.

We share the University's mission to contribute to society through the pursuit of education, learning and research at the highest international levels of excellence.

www.cambridge.org
Information on this title: www.cambridge.org/9781009705233

DOI: 10.1017/9781009705264

© Marie-Eve Desrosiers and Nic Cheeseman 2026

This publication is in copyright. Subject to statutory exception and to the provisions of relevant collective licensing agreements, with the exception of the Creative Commons version the link for which is provided below, no reproduction of any part may take place without the written permission of Cambridge University Press & Assessment.

An online version of this work is published at doi.org/10.1017/9781009705264 under a Creative Commons Open Access license CC-BY-NC-ND 4.0 which permits re-use, distribution and reproduction in any medium for non-commercial purposes providing appropriate credit to the original work is given. You may not distribute derivative works without permission. To view a copy of this license, visit https://creativecommons.org/licenses/by-nc-nd/4.0

When citing this work, please include a reference to the DOI 10.1017/9781009705264

First published 2026

A catalogue record for this publication is available from the British Library

A Cataloging-in-Publication data record for this Element is available from the Library of Congress

ISBN 978-1-009-70523-3 Hardback
ISBN 978-1-009-70525-7 Paperback
ISSN 2515-706X (online)
ISSN 2515-7302 (print)

Additional resources for this publication at www.cambridge.org/Desrosiers/Cheeseman.

Cambridge University Press & Assessment has no responsibility for the persistence or accuracy of URLs for external or third-party internet websites referred to in this publication and does not guarantee that any content on such websites is, or will remain, accurate or appropriate.

For EU product safety concerns, contact us at Calle de José Abascal, 56, 1°, 28003 Madrid, Spain, or email eugpsr@cambridge.org

The Rise of Authoritarian Middle-Powers and What It Means for World Politics

Elements in International Relations

DOI: 10.1017/9781009705264
First published online: February 2026

Marie-Eve Desrosiers
University of Ottawa

Nic Cheeseman
University of Birmingham

Author for correspondence: Marie-Eve Desrosiers,
Marie-Eve.Desrosiers@uOttawa.ca

Abstract: In recent years, a group of influential authoritarian states has emerged that fall between the ranks of great powers and small states. These authoritarian middle-powers – such as Türkiye and the United Arab Emirates – exert considerable influence, particularly in their region. Yet this development has been overlooked in favor of a focus on superpowers, especially China and Russia. We therefore lack a framework for understanding their behavior and impact. This Element offers the first comprehensive analysis of how non-democratic middle-powers engage abroad. Drawing on critical case studies, it shows how the combination of authoritarian politics and mid-level status leads to distinctive foreign policies. In particular, these strategies erode global democratic norms and institutions through a combination of hard power and transnational repression tempered by hedging and legitimation strategies. In this way, authoritarian middle-powers are helping to unravel the liberal rules-based order. This title is available as Open Access on Cambridge Core.

Keywords: middle-power, authoritarianism, foreign policy, world order, international relations

© Marie-Eve Desrosiers and Nic Cheeseman 2026

ISBNs: 9781009705233 (HB), 9781009705257 (PB), 9781009705264 (OC)
ISSNs: 2515-706X (online), 2515-7302 (print)

Contents

Introduction	1
1 Middle-Powers: Why Do We Need a Revised Theory?	9
2 Multilateralism and International Relations-Building	28
3 Power Projection and Foreign Policy	40
4 Nation-Branding and the Ideas and Ideologies Used to Foster Legitimacy	52
Conclusion: Toward a New Research Agenda on Authoritarian Middle-Powers	63
List of Abbreviations	68
References	69

An Online Supplementary material is available at www.cambridge.org/Desrosiers/Cheeseman

Introduction

The current wave of autocratization around the world is changing how billions of citizens experience domestic and world politics, and poses a profound challenge to the global architecture long seen to structure international politics: the liberal rules-based international order. To date, two countries – China and Russia – have dominated explanations of this trend. There is, however, a growing recognition that a much wider set of states shape current global trends away from democratic government and the post–Second World War system. This includes democracies long taken to be stable, such as India and the United States. Given their sheer size in terms of population – representing more than a fifth of all people on the planet – democratic decay in these polities will have a profound effect on global politics and democracy. Yet it is not only great and superpowers that are shaping current trends. A group of less prominent states are also contributing to a shift away from the liberal order at both the domestic and global level. The combined impact of the strategies employed by countries such as Türkiye, the United Arab Emirates (UAE), and Venezuela, for example, sustain some of the world's deadliest conflicts, destabilize regional politics, and undermine the commitment of multilateral institutions to upholding democratic standards. In terms of their wealth and international influence, many of these states fall into the category of "middle-powers" – a term that became popular in International Relations following the end of the Cold War, which is once again gaining prominence.

The concept of middle-power has been the subject of considerable debate, but remains loosely defined and overly focused on democratic countries. At minimum, it refers to states that have mid-level military and/or economic capacity. Such states can therefore be powerful forces in their region, but do not qualify as global major powers. According to George Glazebrook's early framing (1947: 307), these states "make no claim to the title of great power, but have been shown to be capable of exerting a degree of strength and influence not found in the small powers". Scholars have disagreed on whether to define middle-powers solely on the basis of their capabilities or with regard to the behavior they manifest internationally.[1] There has nonetheless been a general consensus about their core features. Traditional democratic middle-powers were seen as liberal internationalists and stabilizers, defending multilateralism and projecting liberal-democratic values abroad to win more legitimacy and international influence (Kutlay and Onis 2021; Sandal 2014). The most studied middle-powers of the 1990s, such as Australia and Canada, were argued to largely act benignly abroad. It is thus no coincidence that classic middle-power theory gained traction during

---

[1] On this debate, see our discussion on definitions in Chapter 1 below. We define middle-powers on the basis of size and influence, since defining them on the basis of their behavior is tautological.

periods when the global order was favorable to the liberal internationalist foreign policy these states pursued, that is, following the end of the Second World War and during the supposed triumph of liberal democracy in the early 1990s.

The countries that have risen to prominence in the last fifteen years have similar capabilities to the classic set of middle-powers discussed by the likes of Andrew Cooper and Richard Higgott (Cooper et al. 1993) but feature one major difference: they are not democratic. This includes states that are clearly authoritarian, such as Saudi Arabia and Türkiye, and countries that are moving away from democracy, such as Indonesia and Mexico. To reflect this, we refer to both autocratic and autocratizing middle-powers, but often simply refer to these cases as "authoritarian" states to avoid repetition.

It is critical to understand how these rising middle-powers operate, especially given their prominence in regions of wider geostrategic significance such as the Middle East. Doing so requires revising traditional middle-power theory, however. On the one hand, while the literature that has developed to explain the foreign policy of countries such as Canada and Norway has valuable insights for understanding their authoritarian counterparts, it is unlikely to fully capture their motivations and impact. Indeed, traditional middle-power theory explicitly made this point: it was premised on the idea that a state's foreign policy and international behavior are fundamentally shaped by domestic characteristics, including regime type. Authoritarian states that are predominantly focused on securing regime survival and deploy repressive strategies to achieve this should be expected to employ a different kind of foreign policy. On the other hand, the international context in which authoritarian middle-powers now operate is very different to that of the 1990s. A decades-long process of democratic decline has emboldened authoritarian strategies and alliances. In today's increasingly authoritarian global context, where a growing number of actors reject the imposition of democratic norms and standards – including countries historically viewed as democratic superpowers such as the United States – authoritarian middle-powers have greater agency.

This trend is further reinforced by the increasingly multipolar nature of the international system. The decline of American hegemony signifies not only a retreat from its role as a standard-bearer of liberal democracy, but also a shift toward a more fragmented international landscape.[2] In turn, this evolving global context affords greater latitude to middle-powers to assert their interests internationally (Abbondanza and Wilkins 2022: 4; Aydin-Duzgit et al. 2025), particularly within their respective regions. We therefore need to revise our assumptions and theory regarding mid-sized authoritarian states' international relations in line with these changes in domestic and international contexts.

---

[2] See, for example, Bekkevold (2023) and Ashford and Cooper (2023) on this debate.

To the best of our knowledge, this Element represents the first attempt to do this systematically from a global perspective. It addresses why and how a broad range of authoritarian middle-powers engage abroad, making an original contribution to an emerging literature that so far has predominantly taken the form of case studies (e.g., Aydin 2021; Aydin-Duzgit 2023; Kutlay and Onis 2021). Building on scholarship on authoritarian endurance and rationalist assumptions about state behavior within International Relations (IR), we argue that authoritarian middle-powers operate in a very different way to their democratic counterparts. Most notably, their drive to ensure regime survival means they seek to foster an international context in which undemocratic politics can thrive. This presents a significant challenge to multilateral norms, standards and institutions, including those related to human rights and democracy. We also show that authoritarian middle-powers often project both hard and soft power in a bid for regime stability and regional ascendance that can destabilize their own regions. The cumulative impact of these trends has the potential to be highly disruptive to global politics, especially if, as projected, the number of authoritarian middle-powers increases in years to come (Cheeseman and Desrosiers 2023). An important corollary of this argument is that these states demonstrate the extent to which domestic conditions shape international behavior, once again reminding us of the complex "entanglement" between domestic and international politics (Putnam 1988).

The Argument

We contend that the survival dilemma faced by authoritarian regimes is more intense than the one faced by politicians in stable democracies: if you lose power, the consequences can be fatal. In the 1960s and 1970s "jail, exile or death" was the "most common outcome for departing leaders in Africa and for more than 30 per cent of leaders in Latin America" (Cheeseman and Klaas 2024: 18). Although the way these considerations play out is likely to vary depending on the type of autocratic or autocratizing state, non-democratic regimes tend to treat retaining power as a zero-sum game in which fewer concessions are made to domestic challengers than in democracies. The policies of such governments are therefore predominantly instrumentalized toward regime survival. Indeed, even foreign aid and peacebuilding, which may be motivated by a number of factors including solidarity and sympathy, are deployed with a view to bolstering the strength of the regime both domestically and internationally. As a result, authoritarian middle-powers' foreign policy is more self-serving, short-termist, and volatile than their democratic counterparts.

Democracies do not always act benignly or coherently abroad, of course. Democratic states have regularly sacrificed democracy and human rights abroad to pursue their national interest, as the authors themselves have documented (Cheeseman and Desrosiers 2023). This is most clearly the case with democratic great powers, which have frequently used coercion and their economic power to pursue their agenda, including in countries as diverse as Iraq and Nicaragua. The United States has also refused to recognize the jurisdiction of multilateral institutions intended to protect human rights, such as the International Criminal Court, especially under the leadership of Donald Trump. Democratic middle-powers have also acted in self-serving and inconsistent ways, though to a lesser extent because acting aggressively in the international arena comes with greater risk of failure and backlash given their limited economic and military capacity. Over the last five years, for example, countries such as the Netherlands and Denmark have moved to cut foreign aid budgets, while explicitly using aid to leverage progress on key strategic goals such as increasing trade and reducing migration.

Our argument is therefore not that democratic middle-powers never act in illiberal ways. Nor are we arguing that authoritarian middle-powers only act in self-serving or harmful ways: some of their actions may be driven by other considerations such as solidarity, religious beliefs, and humanitarian concerns. This is most clearly the case with regard to the role some have played in supporting peace processes and negotiations, which broadcast soft power but are not solely motivated by this concern. Qatar, for example, has played a pivotal role in attempting to secure the release of hostages, most notably through its long-standing mediation channels with the Taliban. The United Arab Emirates has likewise positioned itself as a diplomatic broker, including by offering itself as a venue for sensitive negotiations that other states are unwilling or unable to host.

Rather, we claim that what is distinctive about authoritarian middle-powers is that, because they are more focused on the short-term imperatives of regime survival and have less need to justify such behavior to national parliaments and citizens, they deploy a wider and more unpredictable arsenal of strategies in response to threats to the regime. Scholars have at times called their behavior abroad "instrumental" or strategic (Aydin-Duzgit 2023), at other times "erratic" (Kutlay and Onis 2021); they have also been described as omnibalancers by some, and as aggressive rule-breakers by others. Making sense of these seeming contradictions requires us to understand the delicate balancing act of regime survival.

One manifestation of authoritarian middle-power foreign policy, for example, is the use of hard power to achieve core goals. This has included collaborating with other governments to assassinate dissidents in exile, arming allies in neighboring countries (both partner governments and warlords serving as proxies), and promoting cross-border disinformation and cybersecurity attacks. In some cases, authoritarian middle-powers have also watered down or ripped up security norms and crossed red lines in their regions, which has made them stability spoilers. The Middle East and the Caucasus, for example, have felt the negative impacts of these kinds of strategies from middle-powers such as Azerbaijan, Iran, and Saudi Arabia.

At the same time, the mid-level military and economic power of such states means that governments are constantly aware of the risks of challenging great powers, and of being isolated by operating outside of multilateral institutions. Consequently, they often remain active in regional and multilateral forums, adopting a strategy of hedging in their international relations. Hedging involves sustaining links to a wide range of possible allies and benefactors in order to blunt threats to the government and promote regime endurance. This typically includes joining a range of overlapping international organizations, networks, and alliances, including those headed by democratic states.

Most states engage in some form of hedging and participate in multilateralism, and authoritarian middle-powers are not alone in adopting more assertive foreign policies. However, their behavior departs in important ways from long-standing assumptions about middle-power conduct. While they draw from the soft power playbook to elevate their international standing, they show a greater willingness to adopt coercive strategies more typical of great powers, particularly when regime survival is at stake.

As this summary suggests, the role of authoritarian middle-powers is both important and multifaceted. In a world in which liberal norms are increasingly being challenged, authoritarian middle-powers are adopting a very different type of global citizenship. Where democratic middle-powers were widely seen to play a stabilizing role, their authoritarian counterparts are disrupting the rules-based international order to boost their own prospects of survival, while actively seeking to undermine the brand power of liberal democracy. In doing so, they have the potential to profoundly change world politics in ways that are not always straightforward. To give just one example, in Eastern Africa and the Horn, the UAE has presented itself as a constructive investor and peace mediator, while also fueling one of the world's worst conflicts in Sudan through its support of the Rapid Support (RSF) Forces accused of genocide (Mahjoub 2024).

As the example of the UAE powerfully demonstrates, the destabilizing effect of these states is not reducible to the tendency of such government to align with other authoritarian powers in the international arena. Authoritarian middle-powers consistently demonstrate their own agency and are neither simply pawns of China and Russia nor making up the numbers in bouts of global power politics within institutions such as the United Nations (UN). Their individual actions may be idiosyncratic, but the sum of authoritarian middle-powers' actions on the international scene contributes to the unravelling of the rules-based international order.

How We Make Our Case

We evidence this argument by combining case study analysis with a comprehensive and systematic survey of over 250 academic and gray sources on emerging and/or authoritarian and autocratizing middle-powers.[3] The literature is still nascent and fragmentary and tends to take the form of individual case studies that often use different definitions of middle-powerhood and focus on one specific area of middle-power behavior. Partly as a result, it often comes to contradictory conclusions, with publications focusing on explaining either authoritarian middle-power aggression or hedging, but not the use of both at the same time. We build on this literature to develop a more rigorous definition of authoritarian middle-powers, while revising middle-power theory to develop a new understanding of the core logic driving these states that accounts for both aspects of their apparently contradictory behavior. Our case studies cover some of the most prominent middle-powers, including Türkiye, the United Arab Emirates, and the Like-Minded Group (LMG), which comprises several middle-powers within the United Nations. These paradigmatic cases enable us to illustrate how authoritarian middle-powers operate in specific areas and to demonstrate their impact on world politics.

We present this argument, and structure this Element, in three main parts. The first section addresses the conceptual and theoretical components of our argument. It begins by exploring how middle-powers have been theorized in the classic literature. We briefly revisit these contributions to identify what they can contribute to our understanding of their non-democratic counterparts. We then introduce our own definition of authoritarian middle-powers and our framework for how the logic of authoritarian survival shapes international behavior, including what variations may exist between entrenched authoritarian states and those that only recently started on an autocratizing trajectory. Given that domestic politics fundamentally influence foreign policy, we expect states that are fully

---

[3] Sources were gathered from academic databases such as JStor, Web of Science, and Scopus, and bibliographies of prominent academic sources that had already been gathered from the earlier Google Scholar sources. We thank Daniel Munday for his research assistance.

autocratic to behave differently than states that are in the process of autocratizing, even if they share a similar logic of political survival. This is especially the case for those regimes facing the greatest political survival dilemma, for example, because they lack full control at home. To illustrate the breadth of the playbook deployed by authoritarian middle-powers, we then explore some of the more prominent strategies they use, grouping them into three core areas of international relations: multilateralism and international relations-building, power projection through foreign policy – both hard and soft – and, finally, nation-branding and the ideas used to legitimate state action.

The remaining sections of the Element address each one of these areas in turn. The second section reveals how non-democratic middle-powers leverage different international institutions and forums to advance their authoritarian aims. In addition to looking at formal international institutions, we pay close attention to the informal relations of authoritarian middle-powers, including to what are increasingly being called "minilaterals." The section also provides concrete illustrations of authoritarian multilateralism and relations-building by looking at the efforts of the Like-Minded Group to dilute democratic principles within the UN.

Section 3 focuses on how non-democratic middle-powers project power abroad. We demonstrate that hard power such as military intervention is typically deployed alongside specific forms of soft power, including prestige diplomacy and transactional aid. To illustrate this, we look at Turkish foreign policy under President Recep Tayyip Erdogan, which has blended coercive involvement in Syria with tough diplomacy, and instrumentalized development cooperation to strengthen the foundations of his regime. The section also explores the aspirations for regional dominance of authoritarian middle-powers – perhaps one of the biggest differences to standard assumptions about their democratic counterparts – which makes them potential spoilers of regional stability.

Section 4 then turns to the type of branding and ideological promotion used by authoritarian middle-powers. IR theory has long recognized the extent to which power and influence is based on perceptions,[4] and hence can be shaped by nation-branding efforts, communication, public relations, and (dis)information. We show how non-democratic powers use tools such as nation-branding and forms of identity politics in their international relations, drawing on the example of the UAE and Türkiye. The latter is particularly apposite given that its very name – which was changed in 2022 to highlight a nationalist legacy the government hopes to revive – is part of a broader strategy to recast the country's international image. Through this focus we reveal how the legitimizing efforts

---

[4] This is central to traditions as varied as realism, and social constructivism (see Wendt 1999).

of authoritarian middle-powers, while predominantly designed to improve perceptions of the government itself, nonetheless contribute to shifting global norms, promoting the notion of benevolent or palatable dictatorship.

Finally, the conclusion explores what the ascendance of authoritarian middle-powers means for the global order given that the increasingly authoritarian and multipolar nature of world politics is likely to further embolden such states on both the domestic and international stage. It argues that the recent emphasis on China and Russia's efforts to undermine democratic processes has led researchers, journalists, and policy-makers to overlook the role played by middle-powers. We also argue that it is only when authoritarian middle-powers are considered that one of the key features of the new global order comes into focus, namely that there will be no return to the Cold War. Several recent takes have suggested that the rise of China and Russia means a return to global politics divided between two rival blocs (Abrams 2022). We argue, however, that the competing aspirations of different authoritarian middle-powers, coupled with the fact that they are stability spoilers, suggest that we are unlikely to see the emergence of a stable and unified authoritarian axis. Instead, as recent conflicts and tensions involving Middle Eastern states demonstrate, such as the war in Yemen, the self-preserving nature of authoritarian middle-powers' foreign policy means that their coalition-building efforts will continue to go hand in hand with competition and instability. The future is likely to be more authoritarian then, but also more uncertain and unstable.

1 Middle-Powers: Why Do We Need a Revised Theory?

The development of scholarship on middle-powers is closely tied to the trajectory of the post-War liberal rules-based order. Some of the earliest references to middle-powers followed the end of the Second World War, when a group of liberal-democratic states supported the development of post-War multilateral institutions in the shadow of the great powers (Chapnick 2000; Glazebrook 1947). Following the end of the Cold War and the purported triumph of liberal democracy (Fukuyama 1992), notions of middle-powerhood gained prominence again as several mid-size states began promoting niche global initiatives in support of a reinvigorated multilateralism. During this boom of scholarship, work on states like Canada and Norway strove to illustrate how these democratic middle-powers worked through international cooperation and institutions to promote solutions to global problems.

There was consequently a decidedly democratic focus and Western bias[5] to research on middle-powers up to the late 1990s. It was only later that work on the notion of "emerging powers" began to redress this imbalance, encouraged by the evolutions in middle-power diplomacy itself, such as the emergence of BRICS (Cooper and Parlar 2016; Efstathopoulos 2021). More recently, there has been a growing emphasis on the number of authoritarian states that are middle-powers in terms of their economic size and military capacity, yet act differently to their democratic counterparts. The early "classic" scholarship nonetheless set the tone in terms of debates around what counts as a middle-power and assumptions regarding how these states behave internationally. It is therefore critical to understand this early scholarship to grasp why it does not account for the behavior of states in the authoritarian sub-group.

This section first reviews the conventional middle-power literature and recent work on their non-democratic counterparts before developing our conceptualization of authoritarian middle-powers and setting out the logic of authoritarian international relations. As well as demonstrating the value of a revised approach that understands countries such as Türkiye, the UAE, and Venezuela as cautious yet self-interested international spoilers, we argue that it is important to differentiate between established autocracies and countries that are autocratizing. First, as governments that are not necessarily fully committed to authoritarian rule, autocratizing states have a particularly strong incentive to maintain alliances with both democratic and authoritarian partners. Second, countries that have only recently begun to move away from democracy may still feature some domestic checks and balances capable of shaping foreign policy decisions, complicating the process of using foreign policy as a tool of regime survival.

---

[5] We thank Adam Chapnick for this point.

Finally, we explain why our discussion is structured around three main types of strategies, setting the scene for the sections that follow. In doing so, we are able to show the range of ways in which authoritarian middle-powers are distinctive, including in terms of their approach to multilateralism and international relations-building, their use of hard and soft power, and the kinds of ideas that are developed to legitimate state action. While these strategies are widely used, their specific deployment – and the ways in which they are combined – is characteristic of authoritarian middle-powers.

Conventional Definitions of the "Middle" and Democratic Middle-Powers

At the heart of conventional theorizing on middle-powers lay one basic operating logic: unable to broadcast global power through military might and economic dominance like great powers, mid-size states adopt a different approach to international relations centered around norms, values, and a principled foreign policy. Such strategies were designed to enhance their global influence and domestic legitimacy, while avoiding treading on the toes of great powers. This made defining exactly what qualifies as "middle"-power status essential, but also a source of debate. Scholars of traditional middle-power theory coalesced around two major traditions with regard to defining the concept: a positional camp focused on states' ranking in the global power hierarchy, and a behavioralist camp based on how they operate.[6]

For "positional" scholars, middle-powerhood was rooted in how states' military and economic capabilities ranked in relation to great and small powers (Wohlforth et al. 2018: 527). To establish global power rankings, scholars proposed a variety of measures, from military capability (i.e. prowess), gross domestic product (GDP, wealth) and population (size), to vaguer and harder to assess indicators such as international influence and reputation. Carsten Holbraad's seminal *Middle Powers in International Politics* (1984), for example, combined gross national product (GNP) and population size with military strength to categorize states. The most popular and agreed upon measures tended to be those seen as more objective, especially GDP. A state's ranking was then assumed to determine its place and imprint on global politics. From this positional standpoint, middle-powers were presumed to be influential regionally, but to have a limited footprint beyond their immediate neighborhood, at least in comparison to great powers.

The "behavioral" camp instead defined middle-powers on the basis of how states act. This school was especially prominent in traditional middle-power

---

[6] On these camps, see Flemes (2007: 8).

scholarship immediately following the end of the Cold War, which some called a "heyday of normative middle-power diplomacy" (Nagy and Ping 2023). The behavioralist position rested on the implicit assumption that middle-powers were able to exercise agency and craft their own foreign policy, which they exercise in a similar fashion because they share certain regime characteristics (Efstathopoulos 2021: 385). Given that the states originally studied in the 1990s were predominantly "wealthy, stable, egalitarian, social democratic" (Jordaan 2003: 165), middle-powers were understood to espouse a form of moral global citizenship centered on internationalist norms and collaborative values. Thus, in contrast to the positionalists, the behavioral camp defined middle-powers by starting with foreign policy and working backward – with the implication that countries that did not behave in this way would not be considered middle-powers at all, whatever their wealth and strength.

Neither camp managed to fully resolve these debates, or some of their own internal contradictions. The positionalist camp faced challenges regarding which metric best measured middle-power status, while the behavioral camp was seen as tautological, as the key outcome of interest was also the definition used to identify middle-powers. Despite their disagreements, both strands of literature nonetheless agreed on a number of key points. A key one was the importance of linkages between the domestic and international when making sense of middle-power behavior, including how size and more implicitly the democratic makeup of traditional middle-powers matter to their behavior abroad. For conventional middle-power theory, the drivers of international middle-power behavior have therefore tended to be rooted in two main sources: first, the constraints middle-powers face, whether in terms of capacity or in relation to the space they are left by major powers, and second, the belief that promoting certain international collective goods through an avowedly altruistic foreign policy represented a win-win position.

On the one hand, middle-power foreign policy strengthened their domestic legitimacy because citizens favored prestige diplomacy and aid; on the other, it was good for their standing in relation to other countries and the wider international system. These two factors were particularly compelling because they were self-reinforcing. By acting as "good" global citizens, traditional middle-powers could gain a different kind of influence abroad than that afforded to great powers due to their military might and economic influence, as well as domestic legitimacy from the approval of voters. While different scholars have continued to make strong cases for the primacy of each of these drivers (see Cooper 2011), it is important to keep in mind that it is the interaction between the two that made this kind of foreign policy so compelling for states such as Canada: it seemed both rational and beneficial to pursue a seemingly moral or collaborative foreign policy.

This led such countries to take the international "moral high ground" in spaces removed from the realm of realpolitik occupied by more powerful players. Democratic middle-powers became entrepreneurs in terms of internationalist practices to try and punch above their weight (Cooper 2018). Furthermore, because there is strength in numbers, and democratic middle-powers lack the capacity to force change on their own, they have long been theorized to favor working through alliances and coalitions of like-minded states. Given that informal or ad hoc coalitions risk being taken over by larger powers, middle-powers were typically expected to be particularly keen liberal internationalists and supporters of formal and institutionalized patterns of cooperation, championing multilateral arenas such as the UN that have historically afforded them opportunities to "exercise greater global influence" (Cooper 2011: 318, 330). This emphasis on institutions naturally encouraged a focus on the norms and rules needed for such bodies to work effectively. Democratic middle-powers such as Australia, Canada, or Norway were seen as a constructive component of the international political system, promoting principles of democracy and human rights both in multilateral institutions and in other countries.

By investing in global collective goods, democratic middle-powers deployed "soft power" – what Joseph Nye (1990) described as the ability to co-opt and/or persuade other states to adopt a similar approach without using might or force – in comparison to the geostrategic hard power games of greater powers. This was fitting, because democratic middle-powers' use of soft power stressed their moral authority. Their foreign policy and especially diplomacy have also been described as "niche" and selective (Cooper 1997), as it often centered on specific key global internationalist agendas and initiatives that captured the imagination of democratic elites. Classic examples include international mediation and peacebuilding, the Ottawa Treaty on landmines, and the development of structures to enact international criminal law.

Two major points implicit in the discussion so far are worth bringing out explicitly as they are important for how we understand states' behavior. First, middle-powers' behavior has always been understood as a two-level game: their domestic characteristics shape foreign policy and behavior abroad, and vice versa. As Anna Grzywacz and Marcin Florian Gawrycki (2021) put it, "foreign policy begins at home." Understanding middle-power behavior therefore requires us to understand states' domestic political economy, be it liberal-democratic or authoritarian. Second, and relatedly, the bulk of scholarship on classic middle-powers was produced during a liberal epoch and was tied to key internationalist moments of the post-Second World War order. While some scholars have argued that democratic middle-powers can step up to the plate in times of global uncertainty (Ikenberry 2016; Paris 2019), by and large they are seen to have thrived in stable liberal-democratic epochs. This can be seen as an implicit call to recognize how different international contexts foster different patterns of behavior in states. In today's more authoritarian and multipolar world, a different kind of middle-power is being emboldened.

Developing a more suitable framework for understanding non-democratic middle-powers therefore requires us to take both domestic and international context into account. Emerging scholarship on authoritarian middle-powers is increasingly recognizing this point, while also stressing that traditional middle-power theory cannot fully account for the behavior of states such as now authoritarian Türkiye – one of the most studied non-democratic middle-powers – or autocratizing Mexico. A key theme within this new literature is that authoritarian mid-level states instrumentalize their foreign policy to enhance state stability and regime endurance. In one of the more explicit accounts on authoritarian middle-powers' behavior, for example, Digdem Soyaltin-Colella and Tolga Demiryol argue that Türkiye's "activism" abroad is inherently linked to domestic regime survival (2023). For instance, the regime's investment in drone development and exports serves both to boost national pride and to enhance border security. In a similar manner, Senem Aydin-Duzgit has shown that Türkiye "picks and chooses" how it engages with the European Union, contesting Europe's liberal norms most actively when it is seen as a matter of "regime security and to facilitate regime survival" (2023: 2330, 2321). Türkiye's engagement abroad therefore serves both to legitimate the government through the "populist dividend" it affords (Kutlay and Onis 2021), and to displace or neutralize the challenge that regional and global norms and agreements could pose to the regime.

This framing reflects wider trends in emergent scholarship, which depicts the authoritarian nature of these states as the main driver of their different or "unusual" approach to foreign policy (Kutlay and Onis 2021). Umut Aydin, for example, argues they are prone to retreating from the kinds of spaces and activities associated with traditional middle-powers (2021: 1379). Authoritarian middle-powers have also been described as confrontational, aggressive, and as status quo challengers, especially in their region (Jordaan 2003). Relatedly, a number of scholars have insisted that the distinctive characteristic of authoritarian middle-powers is their use of military force and hard power as opposed to the soft power of their democratic counterparts (Kutlay and Onis 2021; Soyaltin-Colella and Demiryol 2023).

By contrast, a different set of scholars have instead focused on the particularly strong commitment of these states to "nation-branding" activities that are needed precisely to cover-up the regime's domestic and international abuses (Alderman 2024), as well as efforts to reshape the international environment to make it more favorable to their type of politics (Grzywacz and Gawrycki 2021). Aydin-Duzgit, in particular, has called attention to the importance of ideas, diplomacy and image-management and to the way these states seek to influence global attitudes and perceptions, for example through engagement in multilateral institutions (Aydin-Duzgit 2023).

Put differently, many analysts of authoritarian middle-powers such as Türkiye and Venezuela tend to emphasize *either* their overtly aggressive foreign policy *or* their more subtle efforts to undermine liberal international norms through discourse. Both of these "two faces" of authoritarian middle-powers are seen to be driven by their domestic political context (Grzywacz and Gawrycki 2021). The literature on authoritarian middle-powers therefore remains somewhat fragmented. It tends to present these states as either aggressive or cautious, militarized or ideational, with limited explanation of how these different approaches can be made compatible, or how they relate to regime survival.

This has also led to an incomplete understanding of their impact on the liberal international order. While scholars broadly agree that these states challenge the liberal order, they diverge on the nature and extent of that challenge. For some authors, such as Kutlay and Öniş, these states mount a frontal assault on the liberal rules-based order by promoting militarism and unilateralism (2021). For others, the challenge is more indirect: authoritarian middle-powers subvert liberalism by withdrawing from global activism or questioning the legitimacy of international institutions (Aydin 2021; Aydin-Duzgit 2023; Jordaan 2003). In order to build on but also go beyond this existing scholarship, we develop a theoretical framework that explains the tendency of authoritarian-middle powers to simultaneously be more aggressive than their democratic counterparts and to hedge and utilize the power of ideas. In turn, this enables us to provide a more coherent account of the way in which they challenge the liberal order, which includes generating greater regional instability and eroding key multilateral standards and agreements at the same time.

Conceptualizing Non-Democratic Middle-Powers

The majority of scholars and global indices suggest the world has become more authoritarian over the last two decades, challenging the international status quo (Bettiza and Lewis 2020). Several democracies believed to be well-established are in the throes of major crises and many authoritarian governments have continued to entrench themselves (BTI 2024a; V-Dem 2024). The growing number of authoritarian and autocratizing states requires us to ask what their rise means for international relations. As set out earlier, the emergent scholarship on authoritarian and autocratizing middle-powers views these states as operating on a different logic given their domestic context (Akpinar 2015; Sandal 2014). Yet, there remains a lack of conceptual clarity and consensus on exactly how they should be defined.

Authoritarian states in this category are also conceived of as secondary powers, i.e. second to the great powers, rather than minor or peripheral, but exactly what this means is not always clear. Umut Aydin proposes that "in terms of capabilities [authoritarian middle-powers] rank between the Great Powers and the small powers that make up the majority of states" (2021: 1377). While there is consensus that this means that authoritarian middle-powers are often leaders in their region without the capacity to impose themselves globally, there is variation in terms of exactly where the threshold lies between great powers, middle-powers and the rest (Abbondanza and Wilkins 2022). One reason the task of defining mid-level status is particularly challenging is that many authoritarian countries in this category have experienced recent changes in terms of their international standing or influence. Nukhet Sandal, for example, speaks of a "new generation" or "second generation of middle-powers" (2014: 705). Similarly, scholars stress the relatively recent emergence of many of these states on the international scene, using terms such as "emerging" or "rising" (Burton 2021; Ongur and Zengin 2017). For her part, Aydin speaks of states "on an upward trajectory in terms of military and economic capabilities" (2021: 1379–1380). In most cases, there is an agreement that this process began after the end of the Cold War, with a notable surge in recent decades, with the exception of long-standing cases such as Iran.

In order to summarize the most commonly referenced cases, and the discrepancies between some of them in terms of size and capacity, Table 1 shows how some of the countries that are regularly named as middle-powers' rank on the basis of GDP and military spending. For the most part, these middle-powers reside somewhere between the 10th and 50th place globally in terms of their economic power and/or the size of their military sector. There are considerable differences, however, within these categories. Compare Japan, for example, which ranks so highly on GDP it could almost be considered a great power on that score, to states such as Norway and Iran, which have much smaller economies and are closer in many ways to more developed small powers. Similarly, Saudi Arabia ranks 5th in the world when it comes to military spending, whereas Mexico is ranked 29th and spends one seventh as much as a percentage of GDP.

Table 1 How commonly referenced middle-powers rank on selected global indicators

	Country	Global economic ranking	Global military ranking*	V-Dem regime status
Traditionally categorized as democratic middle-powers	Australia	13	13	Liberal democracy
	Canada	10	15	Liberal democracy
	Japan	4	10	Liberal democracy
	Netherlands	17	22	Liberal democracy
	Norway	31	30	Liberal democracy
Categorized as autocratizing middle-powers	Brazil*	9	19	Electoral democracy
	Indonesia	16	28	Democratic greyzone (⇓)**
	Mexico	12	26	Democratic greyzone (⇓)
Categorized as authoritarian middle-powers	Iran	36	34	Closed autocracy
	Saudi Arabia	19	5	Closed autocracy
	Türkiye	18	24	Electoral autocracy
	UAE	29	17	Closed autocracy

Source: World Bank 2023; SIPRI 2022 and World Bank; V-Dem 2024 Regimes of the World and ERT.
* Calculated based on military expenditures (2022).
** Until the end of the Jair Bolsonaro presidency (31 December 2022).
***Arrows indicate an episode of autocratization between 2013 and 2023. 'Greyzones' are "either in the 'lower bound' of electoral democracies or in the 'upper bound' of electoral autocracies" (V-Dem 2004: 11).

Table 1 also reveals that there is considerable variation in what scholars use as the threshold for a country to be considered authoritarian. This is partly because defining authoritarianism is challenging. Democracy and autocracy form a spectrum, with various possible combinations, including a "competitive-authoritarian" middle ground (Levitsky and Way 2010). The universe of authoritarian states thus features more repressive regimes at one end of the spectrum and more tolerant ones at the other. There is also variation between countries with very different structures of government, including military juntas, monarchic or personalist regimes, and single or dominant party polities (Geddes et al. 2014). While authoritarianism is usually defined as a regime that governs by limiting political alternance, controlling access to state institutions, and infringing on human and especially political rights, scholars differ on what level of abuse is required for a country to fall into the authoritarian category.

A further complication that needs to be considered is that some states are autocratizing, but have not yet become fully authoritarian. As shown in Table 1, for example, Mexico is currently regarded as belonging in the democratic category, though it is also believed to be on a steep downward trajectory. The same was true of Brazil during the presidency of Jair Bolsonaro, and of Indonesia since 2009. These states cannot simply be considered authoritarian, not least because they may never breakdown into full-blown autocracy. Yet, it is important not to ignore this category of country, because if the government has begun undermining democratic institutions and values, it has a vested interest in preventing the enforcement of electoral and human rights standards. At the same time, such cases cannot be expected to behave in exactly the same way as authoritarian states, because they may still feature some influential checks and balances.

One final feature of nondemocratic middle-powers that is often referenced by scholars but not included in formal definitions is that most come from what is often called the "Global South." Eschewing debates about what counts as the Global South (is Türkiye Southern? Is Kazakhstan?), authoritarian middle-powers are generally defined as "Southern," "developing," and/or "peripheral" in terms the center–periphery distinction found in dependency theory (Aydin-Duzgit 2023; Soyaltin-Colella and Demiryol 2023). Charalampos Efstathopoulos, in particular, argues that the actions of these states should be interpreted primarily through a Southern lens, rather than one that emphasizes their emerging status because their rise to prominence may not be as linear or straightforward as the notion of emergence implies (2021: 388).

Building on these insights but seeking to deliver greater clarity in terms of middle-powerhood criteria, we define authoritarian and autocratizing middle-powers as states that are regional leaders but unable to exert dominance globally. In order to be consistent and avoid conceptual stretching, we only count a state to be a middle-power if it ranks lower than 10th and higher than 50th globally on *both* military and economic capacity, *or* does not meet this criterion but ranks in the top two countries in its own region in terms of *both* military and economic capacity.[7] We include this latter consideration because although these countries have a weaker claim to be considered second-level powers, and are less able to influence global events, a key feature of middle-powers is that they are locally powerful without being globally dominant. The majority of our discussion focuses on states that qualify as middle-powers in terms of their global ranking,

---

[7] For a longer discussion of the merits and weaknesses of these indicators, please see online appendix.

Table 2 Authoritarian and autocratizing middle-powers

	Authoritarian	**Autocratizing**
Included on the basis of global ranking	Bangladesh* Egypt Iran Pakistan Philippines Saudi Arabia Singapore Thailand Türkiye UAE Vietnam, Venezuela**	Indonesia Mexico Poland*** Romania South Korea
Included on the basis of regional ranking	Algeria Angola Azerbaijan Ethiopia Nigeria Morocco Uzbekistan	****

Source: World Bank 2023; SIPRI 2022 and World Bank; V-Dem 2024.

* Prior to the recent political transition and the fall of Sheikh Hasina.

** The figures on military spending in Venezuela are contested and impacted by sanctions – see online appendix for more details.

*** Prior to the election of Donald Tusk's government in 2023.

**** There are no countries in this category – all of the states that would be considered middle-powers on the basis of the regional consideration also meet the global criterion.

such as Iran, Saudi Arabia, Türkiye, and the UAE, and which have the strongest claim to middle-power status (see Table 2). Also drawing examples from middle-powers included on the basis of our "regional leader" criterion, however, enables us to demonstrate the impact these countries have on regional international relations, and the extent to which they exhibit similar patterns of behavior to more established middle-powers on the world stage.

As our argument only covers non-democratic states, we also need clear criteria to identify authoritarian and autocratizing countries. We consider a country as authoritarian if it has been classified as an autocracy by V-Dem as of 2023.[8] We

---

[8] This category includes all states classified as either a "closed autocracy" or an "electoral autocracy," the two authoritarian subcategories in V-Dem's Regimes of the World database.

consider a state to be autocratizing if it is not already classified as an autocracy, but experienced an autocratizing episode according to the V-Dem ERT database in the last decade (2013–2023). This generates a universe of authoritarian middle-powers that includes Iran and Türkiye, and a universe of autocratizing middle-powers that includes Indonesia and Mexico. (See Table 2; also see online appendix for a categorization of all countries.)

While it is true that authoritarian middle-powers tend to be more Southern than their democratic counterparts, and are often seen as emergent, we nonetheless have chosen not to make this a feature of our definition for two reasons. First, there are clear exceptions to this tendency, such as Türkiye, and so it is misleading. Second, it is unclear that the fact that states are Southern means they share sufficient commonalities for this to be a useful distinction, or to develop a revised understanding of their behavior – which is the aim of the next section.

Theorizing the Logic of Authoritarian International Relations

The characterizations of authoritarian middle-powers set out in the recent literature – as both aggressive and withdrawn, instrumental and erratic – stand in stark contrast to long-standing definitions of democratic middle-powers. Understanding authoritarian middle-power behavior therefore requires us to rethink and reinvent middle-power theory for the contemporary world. While state size continues to shape what is possible for these states, their non-democratic character means that regime survival – not just state survival – takes precedence. International relations and foreign policy, whether expressed through hard or soft power, therefore becomes a flexible tool in service of that goal. Put differently, authoritarian middle-powers use international engagement not only to secure the state but to preserve the ruling elites who control it.

In one of the clearest statements on the mechanisms at play behind non-democratic international relations, Christina Cottiero and Stephan Haggard argue that: "autocrats desire foremost to remain in power, and this motivates their interests in limiting democratic contagion from abroad and political challenges at home" (2023: 3). This speaks to core assumptions regarding the rationality of states in the conduct of their foreign policy in classic International Relations scholarship and suggests a rationale of international behavior that also echoes scholarship on the logic of political survival developed in comparative studies of authoritarian politics. Yet with a few notable exceptions,[9] these two bodies of work have rarely been integrated to explain state behavior, despite sharing a similar focus on the instrumental behavior of governments. We draw

---

[9] One seminal exception is the scholarship on Bruce Bueno de Mesquita and Randolph Siverson on war outcomes and the retention of power across regime types (1995).

on both to explain the drivers of non-democratic middle-powers' international relations.

Comparative politics scholars often take political endurance or survival to be the main driver of politics, whether in democratic states or authoritarian ones. Most researchers explicitly or implicitly assume political leaders are driven by power, that is, to attain it and retain it (de Mesquita et al. 2005: 19; Svolik 2012). Notwithstanding major debates regarding the rationality of politics (Jervis 1976; Nardin 2015), it is therefore common to assume that the game of politics is played instrumentally. Bruce Bueno de Mesquita and colleagues' now seminal selectorate theory is a prime example of scholarship that theorizes this logic of political survival (de Mesquita and Smith 2011), stressing that there are common rules of the political game that apply across the spectrum of polities and that center on ensuring regime endurance. Autocrats may have some advantages here. Authoritarians depend on a much smaller group of individuals to make it to power and remain in power. Thus, while autocrats never rule alone, the number of constituencies they must cater to and their "minimum winning coalition" is much smaller than for democrats.

Yet authoritarian leaders also play for higher stakes. Although politics is a long-term multi-iteration game, authoritarian governments cannot assume that they will have an opportunity to regain power in the future if they lose it in the present. Autocrats often persecute and prosecute their rivals and may also assassinate them or send them into exile (Cheeseman and Klass 2024). This ensures that the survival dilemma autocratic leaders face is an intense one. It also makes questions of how to win the support of key constituencies a survival imperative (Cheeseman and Fisher 2019), even when elections are not held. The zero-sum nature of authoritarian politics is what motivates the strategizing of leaders to incentivize support, disincentivize defections, and reduce dissent more broadly (Gerschewski 2023).

The higher stakes involved in repressive regimes means that the authoritarian political game is also likely to be played using a wider range of strategies to ensure power is not lost. This tendency is reinforced by a context where regimes not only have the means to bend the rules but face fewer barriers and punishments to doing so. This means that strategies such as violent repression, identity or personalist politics, and corruption are common. Despite this, however, repression and cooptation are rarely sufficient on their own, not least because these strategies can be immensely costly both financially and to a leader's reputation (Cheeseman et al. 2025). Scholars such as Johannes Gerschewski (2023) have stressed how autocrats are keenly aware of the need to persuade larger segments of society to avoid making them into potential challengers. They therefore use legitimization strategies, such as showcasing their ideology, claiming performance or banking on charismatic or traditional sources of legitimacy, to contribute to their political survival. Persuasion is a fundamental strategy of authoritarianism.

This set of assumptions within political science echoes a standard practice in International Relations. There is a long tradition in IR literature of treating decision-makers – or the state itself as the aggregate of government decision-making – as rational actors who deploy foreign relations in instrumental ways.[10] It is true that there has been a vibrant debate about how deep rationality runs, from proponents of rationality as a fundamental assumption to those who qualify absolute rationality assumptions and stress the impact of imperfect information or emotions, for example (David 2023; Yarhi-Milo 2023). Yet dominant IR theories and especially realism, neorealism, neoliberalism, and their variants all consider that states act rationally internationally to gain or preserve power, weight, and influence, or to basically survive in a highly competitive international environment. Put differently, the drive behind foreign policy is to ensure the state does not falter, whether it be democratic or authoritarian.

The major difference between how democracies and non-democratic regimes operate abroad therefore lies not in their core goal but in how they process decisions and how they understand what will best enable them to attain this goal. Rational behavior is not determined by the inherent rationality of a particular course of action in itself (alliances, cooperation, war, for example), but by the decision-making process that leads to the type of foreign policy or international approach adopted. These deliberations are grounded in "credible theories" or what could be considered the logic of a decision. In other words, states hold "credible theories about the workings of the international system and use them to understand their situation and determine how best to navigate it" (Mearsheimer and Rosato 2024).

We draw on these two bodies of literature to build our theory of authoritarian middle-power international relations. Those who deliberate and design foreign policy are state decision-makers. As Bruce Bueno de Mesquita and Alastair Smith put it, "[s]tates don't have interests. People do" (2011: 25). The preeminent driving logic for autocratic leaders is their political survival, and how international relations can be put in the "service of the prince." While authoritarian middle-powers lack the influence of greater powers, they have enough to use international relations as a potent tool of regime survival. This includes pre-empting potential challenges to the regime, diverting attention away from

---

[10] Rational behavior could be defined as "making sense of the world for the purpose of navigating it in the pursuit of desired goals" (Mearsheimer and Rosato 2023: 2; 2024).

embarrassing aspects of domestic politics, and building coalitions that support power retention.

International relations can impact a regime's ability to endure in direct and indirect ways. Directly, foreign states can provide support such as trade, resources, technological assistance, and military hardware that can be used to repress domestic opponents. Forming alliances with powerful states can also help to insulate an autocratic regime from international interventions to (re)establish democratic rule, such as sanctions and support to pro-democracy leaders. Indirectly, achievements on the international stage can be used to legitimize a government back home. Manifestations of prestige and influence abroad, or recognition by other states of a country's prestige or legitimacy, can impact on how it is perceived domestically, making it easier to retain power.

Türkiye under President Recep Tayyip Erdogan offers a compelling example of how authoritarian middle-powers instrumentalize international relations and foreign policy. Following a period of autocratization beginning in the mid-2000s, Türkiye is now widely considered authoritarian. Over the past decade, its international posture has grown markedly more assertive, including military interventions in the Syrian civil war targeting the Kurdistan Workers' Party (PKK). Simultaneously, Türkiye has expanded its role as a diplomat and donor, particularly to Muslim-majority countries – moves that have bolstered Erdogan's domestic image as a powerful global actor. For example, Türkiye is now ranked third in the world in terms of its number of diplomatic missions, surpassed only by China and the United States (Kutlay 2025).[11] This international activism has supported Erdogan's promotion of Turkish nationalism and the vision of Türkiye as a "great nation, and great power" (Fradkin and Libby 2013), a narrative also reinforced through popular cultural products like the nationalist, neo-Ottoman TV series *Diriliş: Ertuğrul*, which glorifies the country's imperial past. Erdogan also cultivated strategic ties abroad, including with President Donald Trump, securing US support for the flawed 2017 constitutional referendum and 2018 presidential elections. This undermined the credibility of international election observers and helped deflect democratic criticism. In this way, Erdogan's leadership epitomizes the use of more assertive foreign policy strategies to enhance a leader's legitimacy, promote pro-regime narratives, and insulate the government from external democratic pressures.

At the same time, however, the leaders of authoritarian middle-powers are aware of the dangers of being perceived to be a threat to global powers, and the heightened risks involved with operating independently of multilateral

---

[11] See also the Global Diplomacy Index: https://globaldiplomacyindex.lowyinstitute.org/country_ranking.

institutions. Consequently, they often remain active participants in regional and multilateral forums that offer a degree of protection. Similarly, these states frequently hedge by joining multiple overlapping international networks and alliances, including those led by democratic nations. This hedging sometimes goes hand in hand with the use of more coercive forms of foreign policy, especially with regard to smaller and middle-powers in their region. Driven by the imperative of survival, some authoritarian middle-powers have not hesitated to employ the full range of strategies at their disposal, including military support for allies in neighboring areas or efforts to establish regional dominance, which bolsters their influence over regional politics and, by extension, enhances their chances of survival. Their behavior abroad therefore often blends hard power with the more traditional soft power tools commonly associated with democratic middle-powers, mixing strategies of regional ascendance with prestige diplomacy, foreign aid designed to strengthen international alliances, and/or nation-branding.

The pre-eminence of political survival is also key to understanding the different strategies adopted by autocratizing middle-powers. Autocratizing states, while moving toward more exclusionary forms of governance, are nonetheless likely to be more constrained by checks and balances institutions, civil society and public opinion, than their authoritarian counterparts. Put another way, they are likely to cater to a larger winning coalition, and to face greater constraints on domestic and international rule-breaking. Judiciaries, for example, have in some cases proved able to serve as a break on autocratization, even in cases of pronounced democratic backsliding. As a result, autocratizing middle-powers are likely to be more cautious in their choice of approach, both domestically and internationally.

We expect this to manifest as more expansive hedging – that is, as we explain below, catering to a more diverse set of international allies, and participating in a wide range of international arenas. Autocratizing middle-powers are also more likely to be more restrained in using international strategies that cross red lines, unless faced with a domestic crisis. In keeping with this distinction, the type of ideological and legitimation registers used by autocratizing states is likely to differ from fully authoritarian regimes. In their extensive survey of non-democratic governments' legitimation strategies, Christian Von Soest and Julia Grauvogel (2017) suggest that autocratizing regimes tend to focus their ideological work on stressing their relations to society, while closed authoritarian states work on ideas that promote forms of identity and solidarity geared toward the regime (personalism or a foundational myth, for example). Autocratizing middle-powers are therefore likely to manifest a form of behavior that lies between democratic and authoritarian middle-powers. At the same time, the fact that they are moving at different speeds toward authoritarianism and experiencing significant changes in regime type means that their strategies may be more unpredictable and that there is likely to be greater variations in approaches among the countries in this category.

As this discussion makes clear, we do not claim that the individual strategies authoritarian middle-powers deploy are all unique. Most states hedge, cultivate alliances, and invest in their international image. Nor are authoritarian regimes alone in adopting assertive or aggressive strategies. What sets them apart, however, is the arsenal of strategies they use simultaneously, and how they combine them to serve regime survival. When compared to their democratic counterparts, authoritarian middle-powers are more likely to use hard power when confronting threats. In addition to departing from the good citizenship described in classic middle-power literature, this behavior also challenges the status quo, crosses red lines, and defies established norms when regime security is at stake. These moves are not accidental but calibrated – harsh where needed, restrained where strategic – to ensure both survival and international maneuverability. In line with this calibrated approach, these states also offset this more aggressive strategy with softer tools, because they need to use regional diplomacy, multilateral engagement, and charm offensives to a greater extent than authoritarian superpowers.

As with their domestic policies, the international relations of authoritarian middle-powers are therefore pragmatic, self-serving and "transactional" (Kutlay 2025). This often results in edgier behavior than is typically expected from middle-powers: bending or breaking international rules, when necessary, with potentially greater harm to regional peace and stability than their democratic counterparts. Their behavior is also more volatile. These regimes enjoy more domestic leeway to shift foreign policy in response to emerging challenges, yet balance assertiveness with other strategies. What some have termed the "erratic" nature of undemocratic middle-powers is in fact a structural function of both their domestic politics and level of power. The efforts of these states to weaken liberal global norms are often bold, especially in their neighborhoods, but only where they can afford to be.

A final important consideration is that foreign policy is shaped not only by regime type but also by the international context. Authoritarian middle-powers are more likely to deploy their full strategic arsenal in international environments that are more facilitative of non-democratic approaches. This is the case today, when the emergence of an increasingly authoritarian global landscape and growing multipolarity have emboldened leaders to pursue illiberal strategies at home and abroad. But our current illiberal epoch is not unique in this sense. The interwar period similarly saw a surge in authoritarianism, empowering illiberal middle-powers like Germany and Italy – with disastrous consequences for global stability. These parallels underscore that middle-power behavior is not fixed. It evolves with shifts in the global balance of power and the normative environment, making it essential to analyze such actors within their broader geopolitical moment. It is in the present context, in which the costs and risks associated with undemocratic behavior have become lower and continue to fall, that authoritarian middle-powers are most likely to engage in behaviors that align with the efforts of leading anti-democratic states such as China and Russia to undermine the liberal world order.

Again, this does not mean that imply that all behavior by authoritarian middle-powers is self-centered, or that they do not act at times in order to promote the greater good, but rather that based on these theoretical foundations we expect these short-term domestic considerations to be a particularly powerful determinant of foreign policy. Moreover, our goal is not to show that the global strategies adopted by authoritarian middle-powers are always effective at ensuring regimes endure, but instead to demonstrate how domestic considerations shape international strategies and to highlight some of their consequences. The trajectory and fate of regimes often diverge from what their leaders expect, and the best laid plans can go awry. The main focus of this Element is therefore not authoritarian survival, but rather to explain how the quest for survival shapes foreign policy, and how the cumulative impact of such strategies has helped create a more inhospitable international environment for the promotion of democratic norms and for the liberal rules-based order.

The Authoritarian Middle-Power Toolkit

We outline the broad contours of the authoritarian middle-power "toolkit" (Schatz 2009) in Table 3 which summarises the key differences set out above between democratic and non-democratic middle-powers. In doing so, we categorize the strategies deployed by middle-powers into three heuristically distinct but by no means unconnected categories: multilateralism and relations-building, power projection and foreign policy, and nation-branding and the ideas and ideologies used to foster legitimacy abroad. These categories have been selected because they echo some of the key characteristics of traditional middle-power behavior – supporting multilateralism, their distinctive use of soft power, the way they promote democratic norms – while enabling us to illustrate how non-democratic states diverge from their democratic counterparts.

These categories also capture three of the core components of international politics: relations between international actors, power (i.e. the ability to influence or persuade others), and legitimizing ideas and ideologies, which emerging

Table 3 A typology of middle-power strategies

	International strategies by type		
	Multilateralism and relations-building	**Power projection and foreign policy**	**Nation-branding and legitimizing ideas and ideologies**
Democratic middle-power theory*	- Leveraging multilateralism - Coalition of like-minded states - Liberal-democratic "alliancing"	- Soft power - Niche diplomacy	- Liberal internationalism/ liberal democracy - Moral authority, focused on ethical objectives
Authoritarian middle-power theory	- Authoritarian multilateralism - Coalitions/like-minded states, i.e. minilateralism - Omnibalancing and hedging - Transnational corruption networks, diaspora as a beachhead	- Hard and soft power - Regional ascendance and/or domination - Extraversive prestige diplomacy - Transactional aid; corralling smaller states	- Nation-branding - Alternative ideologies - Identity as solidarity building, e.g. religion

* These strategies do not imply that traditional middle-powers necessarily behave for purely altruistic reasons.

work on authoritarian middle-powers has stressed is key to their international relations (Aydin-Duzgit 2023; Kutlay and Onis 2021). Multilateralism and relations-building specifically focus on the type of relations middle-powers seek out and support, from engaging in collective forums to the more informal networks they may work through. Power projection speaks to the means deployed by states to try and shape the behavior of others toward them, including in some of its hard forms, as well as some of its softer ones. Finally, as is now widely recognized in International Relations theory, ideas, from ideologies to identities, also matter in terms of how states behave, and how actors behave towards them. This category of strategies therefore centers on the types of notions states promote of themselves, generally in the form of branding or their international identity.

In the following sections we provide empirical evidence to support the characterization set out in Table 3 and explore the different combinations of strategies that states deploy. For each type of strategy, we also assess the impacts of authoritarian middle-powers on regional and global political dynamics. Some of these effects are relatively direct and observable – for instance, enhanced regional coordination in the repression of political opposition, or the destabilization caused by interventionist behavior in neighboring states. Other forms of influence, however, are more diffuse and difficult to quantify. In particular, the sustained promotion of authoritarian alternatives to liberal democracy, or the deployment of nation-branding strategies by repressive regimes to render their models more palatable, generate subtler yet significant normative shifts.

As longstanding debates in International Relations suggest, the ideational, discursive, and normative dimensions of international influence are notoriously challenging to measure. We acknowledge this analytical limitation while nonetheless using a range of sources, including survey data, media coverage, and scholarly literature, that demonstrates the direct and indirect effects of these efforts. One illustrative trend, for example, is the documented decline in references to "democracy" in multilateral spaces. As Jennie Barker demonstrates (2024), the growing tendency to erase "democracy" is a direct consequence of the efforts of authoritarian middle- and great powers to dilute established norms of democratic governance and human rights in key forums such as the United Nations. Importantly, these developments are not merely rhetorical. As we show throughout the Element, by eroding the liberal normative foundations upon which much of the post-War international order rests, authoritarian states aim to render international intervention to assert and defend liberal principles less likely. In turn, this challenges core IR assumptions that view undemocratic states as unlikely to engage in multilateral environments – and necessitates a deeper look at the foreign policy of authoritarian middle-powers.

2 Multilateralism and International Relations-Building

Democratic middle-powers have long been cast as staunch supporters of multilateralism, particularly liberal international institutions. In the context of a more liberal internationalist era, scholars such as Edward Mansfield and Jon Pevehouse argued that multilateralism served as a conduit for democratic norms and even democratic change (Mansfield and Pevehouse 2006; Pevehouse 2005). Conversely, it has often been argued that authoritarian powers tend to be isolationist and are much less likely to focus on multilateral arenas and alliance formation (Aydin 2021). As the previous section has demonstrated, these assumptions about authoritarian middle-powers are dangerously wrong. Authoritarian and autocratizing middle-powers have neither rejected nor disengaged from multilateralism. Instead, they regularly engage international institutions to advance regime interests.

At the global level, including within the UN, authoritarian middle-powers have worked to dilute liberal norms, while using regional organizations – both longstanding and newly formed – to promote authoritarian counter-norms and practices (Cooley 2015: 49). In this sense, they appear to uphold the multilateral status quo through formal engagement, while simultaneously subverting it from within. Beyond formal institutions, they also operate through informal mechanisms, such as minilaterals and ad hoc coalitions with like-minded states. Autocratizing regimes often mirror these patterns, though they tend to be more ambivalent toward weakening multilateral structures, especially in the early phases of democratic erosion.

This section begins by examining how authoritarian middle-powers engage multilaterally, before turning to their international alliances, networks, and finally the transnational relationships they leverage to support long-term regime survival. Evidence from case studies such as the UN Human Rights Council (UNHRC), along with data on the rise of authoritarian regional organizations, reveals how non-democratic middle-powers use these arenas to erode democratic norms and construct spaces of authoritarian coordination and solidarity. While some of these initiatives have been led by global authoritarian powers – particularly China and Russia – we show that middle-powers often pursue such strategies independently, sometimes advancing authoritarian alternatives without direction or encouragement from more powerful allies.

International Organizations

International organizations have long been viewed as central pillars of the post-Second World War liberal order, enabling Western states to promote democratic values and collective security. As regularized forums for cooperation and norm-setting, institutions such as the UN, the European Union, and various regional bodies have been seen by liberal theorists as foundational to global stability and collaboration (Ruggie 1992). Yet these same organizations – most notably the UN Human Rights Council (UNHRC) – have become arenas of contestation, where authoritarian states promote counter-norms that align more closely with their regimes. This includes advancing principles such as sovereignty and non-intervention, limiting scrutiny of authoritarian practices, and denying support to pro-democracy actors.

While China has often led these efforts, it has not acted alone. Authoritarian middle-powers – including Egypt, Saudi Arabia, and Venezuela – have played key roles in reshaping multilateral spaces to favor non-democratic norms (Inboden 2019). Within the UNHRC, for example, they have backed China's push to redefine human rights in developmental terms, emphasizing the right to development over political freedoms (Ginsburg 2020; Piccone 2018: 4). In some instances, this norm revisionism has also extended to promoting conservative, "traditional" values with adverse consequences for women's and LGBTQI+ rights (Cooley 2015: 50–53).

Along with China and Russia, middle-powers have also argued for understanding multilateralism through the lens of civilizational diversity and global equity. This includes the speech by President Maduro of Venezuela at the UN General Assembly arguing for a new world that ends "old hegemonies, to put an end to the pretense of some to become policemen and judges of all the peoples of the world,"[12] and President Erdogan's demand to make the world "bigger than five" in reference to the Security Council.[13] These efforts at changing some of the classic liberal underpinnings of the UN have also gone hand in hand with attempts – not always successful – to change practices associated with the defense of democratic and liberal norms. This has predominantly focused on minimizing criticism leveled at specific authoritarian or autocratizing states for their human rights record within multilateral institutions and constraining the participation of democracy and human rights allies such as non-governmental organizations (NGOs) in such forums.

The informal but influential Like-Minded Group (LMG) within the UN has been a key player in this regard. Originally formed in the 1990s within the then UN Human Rights Commission in response to the Optional Protocol to the Convention against Torture (Inboden 2019: 1; 2021), the LMG re-emerged in 2011 to coordinate like-minded states frustrated by the dominance of more traditional Western democracies at the UN.[14] It now comprises close to

---

[12] September 2021, available online: https://news.un.org/en/story/2021/09/1100822.
[13] Speech delivered at the 78th session of the UN General Assembly.
[14] See, for example, an Egyptian UN diplomat's description of the LMG, available online: https://www.universal-rights.org/like-minded-group-lmg-speaking-truth-power/.

thirty informal members, and middle-powers such as Venezuela, Kazakhstan, Indonesia, and Egypt are core participants,[15] in addition to China and Russia. Through consistent solidarity voting and diplomatic overtures to a wider set of countries, this group has challenged democratic norms and practices and sought to curb criticism of authoritarianism within the world body. Within UN arenas, for example, the LMG has emphasized the need to recognize non-interference as a fundamental principle of international relations, no matter what the conditions in different states. It has also sought to replace the focus on human rights with a focus on socioeconomic rights, criticizing the practice of scrutinizing human rights abuses in individual countries as "'naming and shaming', 'confrontational', 'biased and politically motivated'" (Inboden 2019: 5). This position is perhaps best summarized by a statement delivered by Egypt in 2014, seen to reflect the LMG's core manifesto, which not only calls for the respect of sovereignty but also stresses the importance of recognizing "the social differences, religious, legislative differences between populations" and adopting a greater focus on the "right to development" (Inboden 2019: 4).

More specialized multilateral institutions, such as those devoted to security, have also been a space in which authoritarian middle-powers have pursued censorship and repression, subverting global law enforcement mechanisms for their own ends. One striking example is Interpol's Red Notice system, which allows countries to flag specific individuals to law enforcement agencies so that they can be arrested and, possibly, extradited. This system is designed to enable countries to flag notable criminals but has increasingly been used by states such as Türkiye and Venezuela to harass and control the movements of opposition leaders and dissidents abroad, including via collaborations with the law enforcement agencies of allied states (Lemon 2019). On January 13, 2025, for example, the Government of Venezuela requested a red notice for opposition leader Leopoldo Lopez. In reality, Lopez had committed no crime but had come to play a prominent role in raising international awareness of democratic abuses in his home country, including the manipulation of the 2024 presidential elections, since being forced into exile in 2020. As a result of this subversion of the system, the number of red notices has dramatically increased in recent years, threatening and restricting the freedom of movement of diasporic dissidents.

In response to growing pushback from democratic states against the manipulation of the Red Notice system, authoritarian middle-powers have recently turned to subverting other mechanisms of multilateral police coordination, such as the Stolen and Lost Travel Document mechanism (SLTD). Flagging that

---

[15] The LMG is not based on permanent membership, nor does it require its members to vote with the group, but members have been shown to coordinate activities.

a national's passport is stolen or lost in the SLTD database can freeze a person's ability to travel and hence constrain their movements. Türkiye is a prominent abuser of the SLTD system. According to Freedom House, the Turkish authorities "canceled more than 230,000 passports after the [2016] coup attempt in a bid to confine suspected opponents within Türkiye and limit mobility for those already outside the country. The government also reported as lost or stolen an unknown number of passports" (2021b). The latter strategy largely targeted dissidents abroad.

The emphasis in this section on non-democratic middle-powers should not be taken to imply that liberal democracies have always used multilateral organizations such as the UN for benign purposes. Yet, while democratic middle-powers have often been accused of hypocrisy and inconsistency, they have rarely strategized to actively undermine the norms and values identified with such arenas. Perhaps partly as a result, democratic states have been slow to recognize and respond to these efforts. Consequently, some international organizations are increasingly being turned into a space to promote authoritarian practices through support and emulation. The latter process has occurred through the exposing of "recalcitrant member states to new ideas and anti-democratic strategies, and by setting precedents of inaction when even one member models effective anti-democratic strategies for other would-be autocrats in the group" (Emmons 2020: 228).

Authoritarian middle-powers have also made their mark at the regional level, and it is perhaps here that their impact has been the most significant, promoting regional "authoritarian multilateralism" (Raymond and Sherman 2024; Libman and Obydenkova 2018). The type of tactics employed by authoritarian and autocratizing middle-powers within these regional organizations have been more aggressive, supporting the domestic and international aims of governments in three main ways: as conduits for resources to support authoritarian-leaning neighbors; as mechanisms to coordinate the repressive actions and policies of authoritarian neighbors, including in terms of surveying, targeting, or even arresting each other's political opponents; and, finally as tools to enshrine authoritarian norms in the region, informally acting as a space to applaud and legitimize the non-democratic practices and policies of member states (Cottiero and Haggard 2023). Indeed, the work of Anna Grzywacz (2024) suggests that even within regional bodies with less extremely repressive memberships, authoritarian middle-powers have coordinated to weaken tools for human rights monitoring.

This process is perhaps starkest in the case of leading Gulf States, such as Saudi Arabia and the United Arab Emirates (Kneuer et al. 2019; Sabatini 2014). These governments have used similar playbooks to repress dissidents, from changing the law to make prosecuting opponents and targeting NGOs easier to banning dissent organizations. Relations between states has been key to the success of these efforts. Secret agreements between Gulf States that have since been exposed reveal levels of cooperation to maintain political control well beyond that specified in official security agreements (Freedom House 2021a). Some of these deals are bilateral, such as an agreement between the Saudi king and Qatar and Kuwait that prohibited "conferring asylum, refugee status, or nationality to individuals who oppose their homelands' regimes, and bar[red] support for 'deviant' groups or 'antagonistic' media" (Freedom House 2021a). But many of these efforts have been coordinated through the Gulf Cooperation Council (GCC). For example, with the support of the GCC, Saudi Arabia led a military intervention in Bahrain in 2011 to suppress protest at the request of the Bahraini kingdom's ruling family.

A similar story can be told about ASEAN, where authoritarian middle-powers have worked together to delegitimize calls for democratization and coordinate repressive technologies and tactics. Most notably, ASEAN has facilitated the targeting of government opponents across borders. As Ginsburg notes (2020: 50) "Thai dissidents have been 'disappeared' in Cambodia, Laos, and Vietnam, and cross-border extradition seems to be more frequent."

It is precisely to avail themselves of these benefits that the leaders of authoritarian middle-powers have also gone beyond simply subverting existing regional bodies to investing in revitalizing previously moribund organizations or creating new ones. Examples include the formation of the Organization of Turkic States (OTS) and the creation of the People of our America (ALBA) in Latin America (Kneuer et al. 2019: 451). ALBA, for example, was explicitly created by countries such as Cuba and Venezuela and later joined by others, including Bolivia, Ecuador (until 2018), and Nicaragua as an alternative to existing regional bodies. This was deemed necessary because institutions such as the Organization of American States (OAS) were viewed as either too dominated by the United States, too critical of authoritarian strategies, or insufficiently anti-imperial to be viable options to institutionalize regional solidarity. Indeed, the initial agreement between Cuba and Venezuela in 2004 was a direct response to proposals for the Free Trade Area of the Americas (FTAA), a US-backed plan to eliminate/reduce tax barriers. Hugo Chávez, then the Venezuelan president, described the FTAA as a "tool of imperialism" to exploit the resources of the region for the gain of wealthier states.

In the years that followed, ALBA consolidated its position as a safe harbor for authoritarian and anti-American states. Although a number of its smaller members are democratic, all of the largest states are either fully authoritarian or autocratizing. Moreover, the group invited three prominent authoritarian states known for adopting anti-American positions – Iran, Russia and Syria – to be observer members, expanding their global, if small, network. This reflects the findings of recent scholarship that authoritarian regional organization can serve as a "transmission belt" and "learning space" for authoritarian norms and practices (Hall 2023; Kneuer et al. 2019: 451).

Given these trends, it is not surprising that there has been a dramatic growth in the number of authoritarian-dominated regional organizations around the world (Cottiero and Haggard 2023: 2). Immediately after the end of the Cold War there was an increase in the number of democratic regional bodies, but since 2015 authoritarian organizations are in the ascendency.[16] This has created regional spaces more supportive of authoritarian politics and helps to explain why "regional organizations so often fail to show firmness when upholding democratic standards" (Cooley 2015: 57). The impact of these regional organizations should not be overlooked. According to Christina Cottiero and Stephan Haggard (2023: 4), "members of more deeply authoritarian [regional organizations] are not only less likely to liberalize their politics. They are actually more likely to move in the opposite direction by further restricting civil and political liberties."

In part because the repressive implications of these developments tend to be emphasized by researchers, their economic underpinnings have often been overlooked. The use of regional groupings to facilitate economic exchange and access to resources is well illustrated by the case of ALBA. One of the main challenges for ALBA members has been access to fuel. Neither Cuba nor Nicaragua has domestic fuel generating capacity, and their ability to source cheap fuel on international markets has been complicated by US sanctions. In 2005, a year after ALBA was formed, Venezuela initiated Petrocaribe, a scheme to provide preferential access to its vast oil output for allied states. Under Petrocaribe, countries such as Cuba, Guatemala, and Nicaragua could purchase oil at market value, while having to pay less than half up front, with the option to pay the remainder through a seventeen-to-twenty-five-year financing agreement with a low interest rate that only applied if oil prices exceeded US$40 a barrel. In return, participating members were expected to support Venezuela publicly, including rejecting criticism of electoral manipulation, and to contribute to the development of the country. Cuba, for example, provided doctors to offset some of the cost of oil imports. Although this system started to collapse when Venezuelan oil production began to decline due to domestic challenges from 2014 onward, for ten years resource diplomacy through ALBA empowered Venezuela to act as a regional leader and contributed to the survival of its authoritarian allies.

---

[16] Measured in terms of whether the membership is predominantly authoritarian or democratic.

Finally, it is important to note that in some cases authoritarian middle-powers have targeted domestic democratic institutions, multilateral institutions and regional bodies they are not even members of to advance their own agendas. Iran, Saudi Arabia, and Azerbaijan, for example, have been shown to use bribery to purchase support in both international and domestic parliaments. In perhaps the most notorious case, Azerbaijan "laundered a remarkable $2.9 billion through four UK based shell companies in order to bribe members of the Parliamentary Assembly of the Council of Europe in order to water down official criticism of Azerbaijan's human rights record" (Transparency International 2019: 1). The aim of the "Azerbaijani laundromat" was to mute coverage of the violent repression of protests movements and the torture of prisoners (Human Rights Watch 2023), as well as condemnation of heavily manipulated elections. In addition to reducing international criticism of the government and hence making the enforcement of measures such as aid withdrawals and sanctions less likely, these strategies may undermine the institutions that they target. The practice of purchasing political support by corrupting representatives fosters a political system in which key institutions are more susceptible to graft and subversion and, when corruption scandals are reported in the media, erodes trust in politicians around the world.

Authoritarian International Relations-Building

Authoritarian states increasingly cooperate through bilateral ties and informal networks, challenging long-standing assumptions in realist and democratic peace theory that such states are unlikely to collaborate.[17] Countries such as Indonesia and the UAE, for example, actively engage in both formal and informal coalition-building with like-minded states, large and small. These efforts, often referred to as minilateralism, involve small groups of states cooperating on specific issues or regions without the constraints of traditional multilateral commitments (Haqqani and Janardhan 2023). Typically focused on economic or security matters, these arrangements are designed to create external conditions supportive of domestic regime objectives.

Coalition-building has also helped authoritarian middle-powers to extend their influence abroad. Julia Gurol and colleagues (2023) point to how middle-powers have positioned themselves as important nexus points between major powers – especially China – and smaller states, increasing their value to both.

---

[17] A dominant assumption of democratic or liberal peace theory is that democracies are more peaceful towards one another and engage in more enduring cooperation. This implicitly depicts other states as less likely "cooperators" (Mattes and Rodriguez 2014: 529).

Moreover, against assumptions of great power dominance, authoritarian networks have often been spaces in which middle-powers have been able to exert agency by promoting new strategies of mutual advantage. Türkiye, for example, successfully proposed the idea of a Trans-Caspian International Transport Route (TITR) or Middle Corridor to link markets across Central Asia, the Caucasus, all the way to China, showing its entrepreneurial side in a setting often taken to be dominated by Beijing.

As the example of Türkiye's Middle Corridor demonstrates, authoritarian middle-powers do not simply prioritize authoritarian coalition-building over other forms of international engagement. Instead, they are "omnibalancers" who play all sides, as convenient, from engaging with democratic allies and international institutions to maintaining relations with authoritarian peers. Some states like Iran and Venezuela have chosen starker and more trenchant foreign policies, but these cases are the exceptions to the norm. Far more authoritarian middle-powers invest in relations with democratic powers and pro-democratic – at least ostensibly – multilateral institutions. Developments that are seen to threaten the regime's existence may call for one-sided or firmer positioning, and autocratizing middle-powers facing conflictual domestic settings are less likely to adopt a traditional "internationalist" approach (Grzywacz and Gawricky 2021), but the default modus operandi is to hedge to maintain flexibility and protection.

Türkiye's ambivalent foreign policy toward Europe and the West exemplifies authoritarian middle-power hedging. Strong enough to adopt antagonistic positions when necessary, Türkiye nonetheless remains constrained by its dependence on key economic and security ties. Threatening not to approve Sweden's NATO bid, for instance, proved to be an effective way to extract concessions regarding potential threats – including Sweden taking action against Kurdish movements – but stopped short of seriously jeopardizing relations with NATO allies. Such hedging is particularly visible in states straddling democratic and authoritarian spheres or world regions, like Mexico and Indonesia (Aydin 2021). This pattern suggests that participation in authoritarian alliances often reflects pragmatic calculations rather than deep institutional commitment or ideological alignment – making such international relations productive, while also unstable and unpredictable (Edström and Westberg 2020).

Finally, it is important to note that non-democratic middle-powers also employ less formal international relations to strengthen their political control back home, such as impromptu bilateral and transnational exchanges and leveraging their diasporas. As Freedom House has argued, "the majority of transnational repression cases involve collaboration between the host and origin states. Security agencies often work together to detain and render targeted activists, and courts and migration agencies fulfill requests to extradite or expel them" (2022: 10). This was the case in the collaboration between Kyrgyzstan and Türkiye regarding the abduction of Orhan Inandi, a Turkish-Kyrgyz citizen Ankara accused of ties to the Fethullah Gülen movement that Türkiye sees as a terrorist organization and blames for an alleged coup attempt in 2016. On the basis of these ties, Inandi was extradited to Türkiye in 2021, where he was subsequently sentenced to jail on terrorism counts. Saudi Arabia has also collaborated with other states to target regime dissidents abroad. In two instances, dissidents were arrested by their host states, Qatar and Kuwait respectively, and sent back to Saudi Arabia (Freedom House 2021a). In the case of Qatar, Mohammad Abdullah al-Otaibi, a human rights defender, had even obtained refugee status after fleeing Saudi Arabia and was arrested as he was about to fly to Norway to be resettled.

A number of authoritarian middle-powers have also worked hard to silence critical voices in the diaspora, repressing "their populations outside their borders as part of their foreign policy" (Dukalskis et al. 2022: 2). At the same time, by leveraging transnational diasporic relations these states seek to amplify pro-regime sentiment abroad. The Erdogan government, for example, has funded pro-regime diasporic groups and Turkish youth living aboard to "strengthen its power domestically and extend the country's influence globally" (Döcü and Daser 2024). The Turkish diaspora is particularly significant to the regime's survival because it has the right to vote in Turkish elections and has become an important pro-regime bloc, with Erdogan winning more than two-thirds of the ballots cast in countries such as France and Germany.[18] As a result, pro-regime elements of the diaspora receive funding to promote pro-government narratives on social and traditional media, and hold events that are designed to highlight Türkiye's successes.

These strategies have often generated considerable tensions with host states because President Erdogan's efforts to mobilize the diaspora in his favor have seen him embrace strategies of radicalization. This has included emphasizing "the idea that there are ontological differences between the Turkish (and Muslim) diaspora" and describing the assimilation of Turkish migrants into the societies of other states as "a crime against humanity."[19] The strained relations with a number of European governments that this approach has generated are another important reminder that while authoritarian middle-powers are hedgers, they will adopt more aggressive and destabilizing strategies when they perceive that core regime interests are under threat.

---

[18] https://www.swp-berlin.org/publikation/the-turkish-diaspora-landscape-in-western-europe.
[19] *Ibid.*

The Impact of Authoritarian International Relations-Building

Assessing the impact of these strategies on the durability of authoritarian states, and their international influence, is complicated by a number of factors. First, it is likely that what is known about the institutional mobilizing, lobbying, and corrupt networks of authoritarian middle-powers is a small proportion of their overall activities. Much like the states that form them, authoritarian regional organizations do not have reputations for transparency or accessibility, and governments naturally hide criminal acts such as interstate repression and cross-border corruption. Second, it is challenging to identify the causal process that led states and international organizations to adopt certain policies and the impact of these strategies. Both the domestic sustainability of governments and their international weight are shaped by a wide variety of factors, and while international strategy is an important component of this, it is not the only one.

This caveat notwithstanding, it is clear that authoritarian middle-powers – in conjunction with influential partners such as China and Russia – are having significant effects on international relations. Within international bodies, such as the UN, they have been reshaping and pushing back against international norms intended to promote deeper forms of cooperation, as well as more international oversight. Many of the efforts deployed such as advocating for cultural diversity or non-intervention have been "sovereignty-reinforcing rather than sovereignty-eroding" (Ginsburg 2020: 55). It is the impact of these counter-norm efforts that Barker records in her work on the declining use of terms such as democracy in multilateral spaces that was introduced above. According to Barker, there has been a dramatic decline in the percentage of states speaking at the United National General Assembly that mention "democracy," from around 90 percent of speakers in the 1990s to less than 50 percent today. This is strong evidence, Barker concludes, that the international "norm of democratic governance has weakened" (2024: 33). Along with the declining global power of democracies, and their falling confidence in the feasibility of intervening abroad, the efforts of authoritarian middle- and great powers to both dissuade and block liberal international action and interventions has had a profound impact on world politics.

These processes have impacted on bodies such as the UN Human Rights Council, which has been increasingly politicized by its authoritarian members seeking to avoid scrutiny over their human rights record (Human Rights Watch 2018). While the right of civil society organizations to participate in the Council's proceedings was lauded as an important feature of the organization, repressive states have found creative ways to constrain their input, from complicating their accreditation process to limiting their speaking time and even retaliating against organizations that cooperate with the Council (King and Pousadela 2025). Moreover, there have been no referrals to the International Criminal Court by the UN Security Council since Libya in 2011. Indeed, in many ways this referral represented the high-water mark of the "responsibility to protect" (R2P) doctrine. In the decade that followed, there were far fewer such interventions abroad, despite considerable evidence of crimes against humanity in Myanmar during the Rohingya crisis (Pattinson 2021), and the civil war in Sudan. As other scholars have warned, the UN Secretariat's failure to act to prevent atrocities is not simply the result of not having sufficient early warning capabilities but rather growing opposition by authoritarian states and waning will among their democratic counterparts (McLoughlin et al. 2023). According to the CIRIGHTS data project, which tracks twenty-four measures of rights protection across the world, "global respect [for human rights] has declined over the past decade" (Piccioli 2024).

At the regional level, the growing number of authoritarian regional organizations have "dampened ... prospects for political liberalization in non-democracies" among their members (Cottiero and Haggard 2023: 12) and have strengthened the position of a range of authoritarian leaders. To return to the example of ALBA, the support of the regional body and its leading members played an important role in sustaining the government of Daniel Ortega in Nicaragua. A former Sandinista rebel who initially governed the country from 1979 to 1990, Ortega returned to the presidency in the 2006 general elections, when his Sandinista National Liberation Front (FLSN) won a plurality of seats in the National Assembly. The quality of democracy fell almost immediately, declining from 0.39 out of 1 in 2005 to just 0.03 in 2023 on V-Dem's Liberal Democracy index.

The support of ALBA, and more specifically "Venezuelan oil money," helps explain Ortega's political success (Waddell 2018). When Ortega first took power, his government was boosted by the receipt of "billions of dollars worth of cheap oil" from Venezuela, totaling an estimated $US 3.7 billion between 2007 and 2016. The favorable terms of the deal enabled the Nicaraguan government to provide a consistent flow of fuel to citizens, and to channel the proceeds of the sale of oil into public services. According to Waddell, "Ortega's government spent nearly 40 percent of oil proceeds to bolster ambitious social welfare programs, including micro-financing for small businesses, food for the hungry and subsidized housing for the poor" (Waddell 2018). This enabled him to become the Central American president with the highest approval rating, which in turn dampened public criticism of his growing centralization of power (BTI 2024b).

This section has shown how authoritarian middle-powers challenge democratic norms in international institutions, fuel the rise of authoritarian regional organizations, and bolster autocratic leaders across diverse contexts. These dynamics have not only contributed to the shrinking of global democratic space but also eroded the liberal rules-based order. We have also argued that authoritarian international strategies are generally less consistent than those of their democratic counterparts. Rather than acting as defenders of rules or long-term collaborators with a shared interest in global stability, authoritarian middle-powers are prone to abandon alliances in the pursuit of more short-termist, regime-centric interests. In turn, this erodes the foundations of the collaborative spirit and activity required to sustain the liberal order into the future.

It is therefore important to be cautious with regard to claims that the future will see the emergence of cohesive "democratic" and "authoritarian" blocs, or of a consistent and stable process of undemocratic coalition formation that will gradually establish a new authoritarian global order. While the threat posed by authoritarian states to democratic global institutions should not be underestimated, this narrative misrepresents both the agency and logic of authoritarian middle-powers. It also mischaracterizes the type of threat these states pose with regards to the liberal international order. Authoritarian middle-powers will not always seek the downfall of multilateral institutions and the existing international system because they are "hedgers" and have had considerable success at subverting them from within.

3 Power Projection and Foreign Policy

The ambivalent and at times contradictory nature of authoritarian middle-powers is also evident in the foreign policy they pursue. At its simplest, foreign policy is defined as the strategies a state deploys abroad in its dealings with other states.[20] While it necessarily overlaps with how a state approaches its multilateral and bilateral relations abroad, as covered in the previous section, we address foreign policy separately to spotlight how some of its key aspects, including diplomacy and aid, have been used by authoritarian middle-powers. In particular, we look at how it has been used to project power in the service of political survival. Authoritarian middle-tier states blend soft and hard power in ways that are often hard to predict. While significantly investing in forms of prestige diplomacy designed to position them as actors of international import, these states have also resorted to more aggressive power projection when needed. Put differently, the episodic deployment of state violence abroad, either to support allies or to gain influence, is part of the broader foreign policy strategies employed by states as varied as Pakistan and the UAE.

As we demonstrate in this section, all of these efforts generate benefits when it comes to regime stability. On the one hand, assassinating regime dissidents undermines the capacity and confidence of critical voices and prevents the emergence of organized opposition. On the other hand, securing regional dominance can boost domestic support by fostering national pride, intimidating neighboring governments, and insulating the regime from future attacks from rival states. Moreover, as traditional middle-powers have long demonstrated, prestige diplomacy such as high-profile mediation can strengthen a state's profile internationally, giving it more influence. Under the right conditions, this can be parlayed into greater access to resources and international support for a government's domestic and international goals – including looking the other way when it comes to human rights violations. To give just one example, demonstrating leadership and success on the international stage and developing the capacity to supply other states with military hardware, as Türkiye has done with drones, may attract support and investment from great powers and allies more broadly. It also challenges liberal norms. Most obviously, the increasing tendency to cross red lines in terms of international behavior without consequence has been a real test of the capacity of the rules-based order to curb non-collaborative behavior. This section sets out how authoritarian and autocratizing middle-powers use these different strategies on the international scene.

We begin by addressing hard power, with examples drawn from Iran and Türkiye. The discussion then proceeds to address soft power projection and in

---

[20] On debates surrounding the definition of the concept of foreign policy, see Leira (2019).

particular prestige diplomacy and transactional aid, looking at the behavior of Egypt, Saudi Arabia, Türkiye, and the UAE. On the basis of this review, we argue that the regular deployment of hard power, even if often in combination with soft power, represents the starkest contrast between the practice of authoritarian and democratic middle-powers. The conclusion then reflects on the interaction of domestic and international goals in shaping foreign policy. There are clearly cases where ideological goals matter as much to regimes as strategic calculations, such as Iran's support of allied groups in the Middle East, but we suggest that these are the exceptions that prove the broader rule that middle-power international relations is heavily shaped by considerations of domestic survival.

Hard Power in All Its Forms

Unlike their democratic counterparts, authoritarian middle-powers frequently deploy aggressive foreign policy abroad. Middle Eastern states and Türkiye have in particular used a range of hard power approaches to secure foreign policy goals for regime endurance. Some of these strategies have taken traditional forms, from deploying military capability abroad in geo-strategically important regions to investing in and showcasing military might (Alpan and Özturk, 2022; Ozturk 2021).

Strategic politico-military involvements have often generated direct benefits for the governments that engage in them. One key example is the role of Middle Eastern middle-powers in the Yemeni conflict. Locked in a geopolitical competition for regional dominance and divided by sectarian identity, for example, Saudi Arabia and Iran have supported affiliated groups in neighboring countries, notably Yemen. Saudi Arabia, consistently considered a "closed autocracy" by V-Dem, has a dire record regarding human rights, both at home and in terms of some of its actions abroad. It led an international coalition against Houthi rebels in Yemen, and in Operation Decisive Storm alone undertook thousands of air strikes against the Houthis supported by Iran. Partly as a result, the Saudi-led coalition has been responsible for a vast number of civilian casualties (Christensen 2021: 315). By contrast, Iran not only backed the rebels but armed them, violating a UN arms embargo. In turn, the Houthis have used these weapons to conduct attacks across the Middle East and the Red Sea, and more recently in Russian-backed mercenary activity in Ukraine. A report by the US Defense Intelligence Agency notes that "[b]etween 2015 and 2024, the United States and its partners have interdicted at least 20 Iranian smuggling vessels, seizing ballistic, cruise, SAM missile components, ATGMs, UAVs, and thousands of assault rifles, rocket components, and other illicit weapons destined for the Houthis" (DIA 2024: 3).

The Yemeni conflict therefore shows how the actions of Saudi Arabia and Iran have been driven by the interaction of two different but complementary impulses. First, broader ideological beliefs and global strategies, and a desire to enhance their political position by strengthening their global allies. Second, competition for regional dominance, and the perceived necessity of countering the international ambitions of a rival in one's region.

Similarly, Türkiye's involvement in Syria – which included four armed interventions on Syrian territory between 2016 and 2020 and taking control of territory in Northern Syria, as well as backing various Islamist opposition rebel groups with Saudi Arabia and Qatar during the Syrian civil war – has also served a range of goals. Most significantly, it has enabled Erdogan to influence developments in the wider region by targeting groups seen to be enemies of the state such as the Kurdistan Workers' Party (PKK), while forging new international alliances. From an international standpoint, Erdogan's strategy appears to have paid off: after the fall of Bashar al-Assad the new regime in Damascus aligned itself with Türkiye, facilitating further military actions against Kurdish forces in Syria. Türkiye's exploits in Syria have also served as a valuable domestic political tool for Ankara. As Francesco Siccardi argues, Turkish involvement has helped "Erdogan connect with increasingly nationalistic constituencies and drum up support around key electoral dates" (2021), which explains why the government emphasizes Syrian security issues during electoral campaigns. In this way, the deployment of hard power and greater regional influence can boost authoritarian middle-powers' authority both at home and aboard.

In some cases, armed aggression has been deployed with more far-reaching goals in mind such as regional hegemony (Richter 2020; Verhoeven 2018). Prime examples include Iran and Saudi Arabia, which have both nourished hegemonic ambitions in the Middle East. In turn, this has encouraged their involvement in nearby conflicts, including Yemen. Regional competition can also lead to rivalries playing out in more distant theatres. The larger region around the Middle East and the Horn of Africa, for example, has been a playground for the hegemonic ambitions of a number of Middle Eastern regional powers, such as Iran and UAE (Verhoeven 2018). This has been exemplified by growing Middle Eastern influence in zones of instability in or near the Horn, including Somalia and Sudan.

The UAE is a case in point. The federation, comprising seven emirates including Abu Dhabi and Dubai, has deployed different forms of what might be called military diplomacy to extend its influence in countries such as Ethiopia, Sudan, and Somalia. Emirati military support has been – until recent reductions – central to Somali efforts to fight al-Shabab, an al-Qaeda affiliate, as well as to develop Somali security capacity (Levy 2024). The UAE has also played a leading role in training Somali troops and setting up some of the country's security structures. By contrast, in Sudan, the UAE has been accused of facilitating and exacerbating a brutal civil war by arming and supporting the Rapid Support Forces, the rebel group accused of shocking human rights violations as they fight the Sudanese Armed Forces (SAF). This is part of a broader strategy centered on providing military and economic support to bolster the UAE's influence in East and North Africa, which it considers its proximate region.

Such approaches can be a double-edged sword, however. Greater regional ascendance can also heighten competition with other authoritarian and democratic powers in the region and complicate the ability to omnibalance. Much of the UAE's activity, for example, has been designed in response to the expanding foreign policy ambitions of Saudi Arabia, leading to concerns of an "arms race" across Africa that will prolong domestic conflicts and make them more harmful. Similarly, the Saudi regime's desire to achieve regional influence has at times stood in contradiction to its goal of avoiding direct conflict with major powers and other regional players, contributing to an increasingly unstable situation (Miller and Cardaun 2020). Most notably, Saudi Arabia's security-focused approach has largely been premised on a "policy of exclusion" regarding certain states, including Iran, intensifying key historical divides (Miller and Cardaun 2020: 1521). While advancing their influence through proxies has avoided direct conflict thus far, these authoritarian middle-powers' continued drive for dominance raises the stakes and so increases the risk of future instability.

While regional hegemony is not a realistic aspiration for weaker authoritarian middle-powers, some nonetheless seek greater regional influence. Qatar, for example, has worked to make itself into an influential player in some of the Middle East's civil wars, by promoting coalitions that support the regime's own leanings (Townshend 2020). Qatar has also increased its activities in Somalia, to the great frustration of the UAE.

Armed aggression has not been the only way authoritarian middle-powers have used hard power for their own domestic advantages. Such governments have also invested in weapons development and the expansion of military production, becoming prominent importers and exporters of military equipment and technology. As Table 1 demonstrates, a number of the countries who invest the most in their military are non-democratic middle-powers. These investments could be interpreted as a defensive move, to prepare against a possible attack. Yet military development has also served to intimidate rivals, enhance relations with the providers and consumers of these weapons, and to cater to conservative domestic publics.

According to the Stockholm International Peace Research Institute (SIPRI), countries such as Saudi Arabia, Qatar, and Pakistan rank in the top five globally in terms of their share of arms imports, with the UAE and Türkiye also in the top 20 (Wezeman et al. 2024). This has led SIPRI to speak of "a pattern of rapid military build-ups in Saudi Arabia, Qatar and the UAE over the past 15 years" (2019: 1). Iran has not matched its neighbors in terms of recent arms purchases, in part because sanctions and an economic downturn have limited its purchasing power. It has nonetheless struck a major arms deal with Russia in 2023 – one Tehran claims is "its single largest procurement of military hardware from Russia in over 30 years" (Iddon 2023). In a quid pro quo arrangement illustrative of how authoritarian middle-powers are deploying hard power and weapons as a vector of foreign policy, Iran committed to send drones in return. It also provided Russia with Fath 360 close-range ballistic missiles in 2024, according to US officials (Lopez 2024).

As the Iranian case suggests, authoritarian middle-powers are increasingly playing an important role in arms development, selling military equipment to third party states, including other middle-powers. In Türkiye, Erdogan's government has proved an effective proponent of this strategy, developing its defense technology sector significantly in recent decades and boosting exports of military equipment. This approach has helped bolster Türkiye's standing by turning it into a "major drone power" (Rossiter and Cannon 2022) and positioning the country at the heart of new authoritarian networks emerging in the Caucasus, and North and sub-Saharan Africa. According to International Crisis Group, "[Türkiye's] flagship Bayraktar TB2 drone has proven effective on battlefields in Ukraine, Libya, Nagorno-Karabakh and elsewhere" (2023: 1). Turkish drones were also of critical importance to President Abiy Ahmed during the conflict in the Tigray region of Ethiopia.

As with its involvement in Syria, Türkiye's growing armament sector has generated considerable domestic benefits. President Erdogan has used advancements in the country's military industry to boost Turkish nationalism and rally his supporters around elections. This includes high profile parades during which military hardware is displayed around the streets of Istanbul and flying giant Turkish flags at strategic points throughout the country. The dual motivations for defense development are highlighted by the example of the TCG Anadolu, Türkiye's largest domestically manufactured drone-carrying amphibious ship. In April 2023, just weeks before the country's general elections, the Anadolu was put on public display in the port of Istanbul to advertise Turkish military technology expertise. These strategies played an important role in enabling Erdogan to retain power in a tight election, resonating especially well with right-wing conservative and nationalist citizens.

These assertive power-seeking strategies stand in sharp contrast to the status quo-oriented approach pursued by democratic middle-powers in previous decades and are more akin to the behavior of great powers. In turn, such strategies can be particularly destabilizing, and the tensions and contradictions they generate are not likely to diminish. The decline of US global hegemony and the ability to offset the risk of crossing international red lines by securing the support of great powers such as China and Russia risks emboldening the use of hard power. The growing collaboration between middle-powers in different parts of the world will contribute to this, as it enables technology and resources to be shared. The isolated middle-power regimes of Iran and Venezuela, for example, have increasingly cooperated, including in the defense sector, with Iran sending weapons to the South American country (Humire 2020; Walsh 2020), from armed unmanned aerial vehicles (UVAs) to anti-ship missiles. The overall effect of this process has been a militarization of regional relations that, if the example of Saudi Arabia is anything to go by, has the potential to destabilize regional, and hence to an extent global, security.

Prestige Diplomacy and Aid as Soft Power Projection

Authoritarian middle-powers have tended to offset their use of hard power through the deployment of softer forms of power, which generates lower risks. Soft power diplomacy has, for example, been employed by Egypt (Siniver and Tsourapas 2023), Morocco (Wüst and Nicolai 2023); Saudi Arabia (Gallarotti and Al-Filali 2014), Türkiye (Alpan and Özturk 2022; Ozturk 2021), and the UAE (Krzymowski 2022) to demonstrate their ability to play a constructive role internationally. In this respect, authoritarian states tend to operate in a similar way to their democratic counterparts, that is, by seeking to gain greater influence through engagement in "prestige" diplomacy or transactional development aid. These strategies promise to realize international and domestic dividends without the risks associated with harder strategies. Growing prestige also creates greater opportunities to demonstrate international influence and hence boost public support at home.

Thematic, Cultural, and Public Diplomacy

Prestige diplomacy refers to high-profile international initiatives designed to attract positive global attention and elevate a state's image through novelty and appeal. Among authoritarian and autocratizing middle-powers, this often takes the form of thematic diplomacy (Bennis 2020), particularly on globally fashionable issues, as well as public and cultural diplomacy. These efforts aim to project international influence and position such states as brokers of relations across nations or cultures, enabling them to punch above their weight despite lacking the military or economic clout of major powers. While reminiscent of the niche diplomacy of traditional middle-powers, the public goods promoted by authoritarian actors lack the liberal-democratic orientation of their democratic counterparts. Crucially, authoritarian middle-powers avoid reinforcing global norms that might constrain domestic behavior. Instead, they favor projects in infrastructure, technology, or culture over those tied to democracy promotion or international justice.

One classic form of niche diplomacy pursued by middle-powers has been mediation. This was a role democratic middle-powers consistently played during their heyday in the 1990s, and so it should be no surprise that it is an arena in which non-democratic middle-powers have pursued prestige and positive reputational gains. While China's growing role in international peace processes has drawn significant attention, it is only the tip of the iceberg. Middle-powers like Qatar, Saudi Arabia, and Türkiye have also positioned themselves as essential mediators within their regions. Since 2010, Türkiye has participated in nine major mediation efforts, including between Russia and Ukraine (Seven 2024: 2). In 2024, it institutionalized this role by creating a Directorate General for International Mediation within its Ministry of Foreign Affairs.[21] This strategy reinforces Türkiye's global standing while serving domestic narratives of international stature, particularly as Ankara distances itself from its traditional alignment with Europe. Similarly, Qatar has capitalized on its strategically hedged relations – with the United States, regional powers, and non-state actors such as Hamas – to mediate conflicts, especially between Israel and Hamas. Its ability to convene adversarial parties has made it an "essential go-between," boosting both its international profile and the legitimacy of its ruling elite at home.[22] These forms of global engagement are particularly attractive because they foster the image that the regime is a peaceful and constructive one, masking its contributions to conflict and political instability in other areas.

Authoritarian middle-powers' thematic diplomacy has also extended far beyond the classic middle-power playbook, however. This includes the emphasis of some Middle Eastern states on future technologies. Digital solutions to governance and development challenges, and the provision of support for other countries to develop their own technology, have been at the heart of major international conferences and diplomatic initiatives promoted by these regimes (Fisher 2023). As middle-powers, they enjoy the economic power to

---

[21] Ministry of Foreign Affairs, online: https://www.mfa.gov.tr/resolution-of-conflicts-and-mediation.en.mfa.

[22] https://www.vox.com/world-politics/2023/11/22/23972238/israel-hamas-deal-qatar-broker.

credibly promote their own visions for the future, as well as the international influence to do so. The UAE, for example, has used this type of diplomacy to diversify its relations across the world. Notably, the Dubai Future Foundation has begun hosting a yearly international Future Forum, the "world's largest gathering of futurists."[23] The Dubai Future Foundation was also behind a special report issued in relation to the country hosting COP 28, the major UN Climate Change conference. This diplomatic focus has helped raised the profile of the UAE and also positioned it as a world leader on future innovation.

Sport has also long been used as a way to raise a country's profile and mask authoritarian abuses. Football, tennis, basketball, and athletics are ideal focal points because they have broad appeal and are generally seen to be apolitical – they are also sports that are either in need of funding (athletics) or are constantly looking for ways to expand their markets (tennis, football). Qatar, for example, has engaged in sport diplomacy or what some have called sportswashing (Fruh et al. 2023), hosting high-profile events such as the football World Cup in 2020 to promote a positive and non-political vision of the country. This has not always led to straightforward wins, however. When Lionel Messi lifted the World Cup for his Argentine team in Lusail Stadium, it normalized Qatari culture, religion and history for millions of fans across the world, all the while promoting the Qatari state and its government. Yet at the same time, activists and journalist seized on the poor conditions foreign workers suffered as they built the event's sporting facilities to highlight Qatar's poor record on labor safety and human rights. Other similar examples of states using sport to "detract from illiberal, non-democratic, and/or exploitative practices in their home countries" (Grix et al. 2023) include Azerbaijan hosting the multi-sport European Games in 2015 and Sheikh Mansour bin Zayed Al Nahyan, vice president of the UAE, securing majority ownership of Manchester City football club.

At times, this process has seen authoritarian middle-powers pay lip service to apparently democratic global norms that do not really challenge their hold on power, in an attempt to demonstrate they are respectable members of the international community. A classic example is the promotion of women's political representation, a strategy that appeals to the community of states that have prioritized gender equality (Doğangün 2020), and does not risk regime survival in the way, say, that holding open multiparty elections would. As Yuree Noh and colleagues recently argued "[w]hile occasionally motivated by gender egalitarianism and women's right activism, autocrats' calculations for adopting gender quotas are often more cynical: an attempt to garner international and

---

[23] Dubai Future Forum, online: https://www.dubaifuture.ae/dubai-future-forum-2023.

domestic legitimacy" (2024: 706). This strategy of "genderwashing" has historically been deployed in a wide range of authoritarian states, including small powers such as Rwanda, and so it is no surprise that it has also been employed by authoritarian middle-powers such as Türkiye and Saudi Arabia.

Cultural diplomacy is another impactful yet politically safe form of international engagement. Saudi Arabia, for example, sought to downplay the controversy over its role in the assassination of Jamal Khashoggi, and in Middle Eastern conflicts, by emphasizing its film industry, fashion, and food. This has gone hand in hand with a proliferation of culture-focused agencies in the country, under the Ministry of Culture, and hence state control. According to Eman Alhussain, the Saudi authorities believe that "the emphasis on culture is essential because it can generate revenue and expand the kingdom's outreach" (2022: 4). Put differently, culture is used as a tool to grow Saudi influence in the world.

Similarly, public diplomacy, which encompasses efforts to influence foreign publics, has also been key to authoritarian and autocratizing middle-powers' soft power strategies in contexts as diverse as Indonesia, Saudi Arabia, and Türkiye (Baser and Ozturk 2020; Huijgh 2017). This often includes the use of public relations firms and lobbying to influence both foreign governments and publics (Heibach 2021: 85). A classic example is the attempt of the Turkish government to sway its US counterpart – and through them the American public – on a range of issues including its position on the Armenian genocide. As part of these efforts, Türkiye hired the American public relations firm Fleishman-Hillard on a contract worth more than $100,000 a month, and spent $3,524,632 on lobbying US political leaders and others in 2007/2008 alone, making Türkiye one "The Top Players in Foreign Agent Lobbying" (LaFleur 2009). During this period, professional lobbyists working for Türkiye had more contacts with members of the US Congress than those acting for any other government. As Heibach has argued, in this way public diplomacy can be used to "obfuscate the use of hard-power strategies, or rather the consequences thereof; and to retain and extend the support of extra-regional actors" (2021: 85).

Authoritarian middle-powers are by no means unique in employing thematic and cultural diplomacy to elevate their international standing. Historically, peace brokering has been the domain of democratic middle-powers like Norway, while mid-sized states as politically diverse as Nigeria, South Korea, and Türkiye have leveraged cultural exports – ranging from food to cinema – to establish themselves as poles of attraction and influence. What sets authoritarian middle-powers apart, however, is the combination of this approach with the use of hard power, and hence the way these strategies are used to divert attention from the coercive foundations and ambitions of these regimes.

Instrumentalizing Aid

A related soft power tool deployed by authoritarian middle-powers is foreign aid. The strategic use of aid as a "primary foreign policy tool" has been associated with countries such as Saudi Arabia, the UAE, and Türkiye, which have all developed targeted aid programs to support smaller authoritarian regimes in their sphere of influence (Dipama and Parlar 2023; Farouk 2020). As Alexander Cooley explains, "emerging donors have stepped in to aid countries not serviced by the Western-led aid community. Since ... the Arab Spring, the oil-rich Gulf states have sent tens of billions of dollars abroad and now provide the lion's share of development aid to Egypt, Bangladesh, the Maldives, and Yemen" (2015: 59). This aid is particularly attractive to partners as it lacks the political conditionality commonly associated with "Western aid."

Non-democratic middle-powers are not alone in using aid for foreign policy objectives. Democratic governments have regularly deployed aid in a pragmatic and self-serving manner, especially for security and economic reasons (Cheeseman and Desrosiers 2023). Authoritarian aid tends to be more nakedly transactional, however. Yasmine Farouk (2020) argues that Saudi Arabia has partly given aid to countries like Malaysia and Indonesia in order to be able to advertise its philanthropic work to citizens and external actors, strengthening its global network. As Waldmeier puts it: "[b]y providing financial assistance to these states, Saudi Arabia receives political recognition of its status" (2017: 6).

Providing aid can also empower authoritarian middle-powers by strengthening their allies and reducing the influence of donors seeking to advance democratic norms. Indeed, the rapid growth in aid from a wide range of authoritarian countries means that in some countries the total assistance provided by the OECD's Development Assistance Committee (DAC), mostly comprising democratic traditional donors, has been eclipsed by non-DAC members. In the case of Bangladesh for example, reductions in aid due to concerns about democratic erosion had a limited effect on the government of Sheikh Hasina following increases in financial support from non-democratic states including Saudi Arabia, the UAE, and most importantly India, now rated as only Partly Free by Freedom House.

The Bangladesh experience is far from unique. A similar relationship existed between Venezuela and allied authoritarian governments in Latin America, as noted in Section 2. Meanwhile, Turkish humanitarian assistance to Africa during COVID-19 helped to extend Turkish visibility on the African continent and contributed to Türkiye's image as a benevolent state with an intercontinental reach (Turhan 2023). This "pandemic diplomacy" came amid more consistent efforts on the part of the Turkish government to extend aid to the continent, "driven by short-term foreign policy considerations, such as breaking Türkiye's international isolation and securing diplomatic support from African nations" (Tepeciklioğlu et al. 2023). Türkiye's aid has been seen as transactional because it has been heavily focused on countries with a similar religious and political background that support it internationally, such as Algeria, Libya, and Somalia, and because it has been so explicitly referenced in the country's nation-branding (see Section 4). As part of this process, Erdogan has insisted on the inherent generosity of the Turkish nation, claiming it is the world's most generous donor when measured per capita (Tuyoglu 2021: 6).

In this way, the transactional use of aid strengthens the influence of authoritarian middle-powers regionally and internationally, while also boosting support at home. As the number of authoritarian states increases, and authoritarian middle-powers become wealthier, the extent of these practices, and their implications for global politics, is only likely to increase.

Balancing Hard and Soft Power in an Authoritarian Era

Authoritarian and autocratizing middle-powers' recourse to hard and soft power, and the way they have invested in military capacity, prestige diplomacy, and transactional aid, illustrates how expansive their arsenal has become. It also reveals the potential tensions and contradictions of authoritarian foreign policy. The tendency of middle-powers to hedge in order to protect themselves and reduce risk can be undermined, or at least run in tension with, aspirations to expand regional influence and in some cases to assert dominance in their proximate neighborhood. There is often also a tension between the kinds of soft power that authoritarian middle-powers deploy and their other forms of behavior, which can undermine their global reputation – as with the allegations of sportswashing that marred Qatar's hosting of the World Cup. This means that the governments of authoritarian middle-powers are constantly walking a tightrope, and that miscalculations – for example about just how far harder strategies can be pushed – are likely to result in instability and in extreme cases conflict.

As this suggests, authoritarian middle powers' reliance on hard foreign policy – including a willingness to cross red lines set by the liberal international order – has contributed to a broader erosion of liberal norms, reinforcing the perception that international rules can be selectively observed or ignored. Great powers – most notably Russia in Ukraine – have spearheaded the assault on some of the most foundational norms of the post–Second World War international order. But it has been the actions of authoritarian middle-powers that have lent momentum to this trend, particularly within their proximate regions, where their involvement in disputes and investment in defense capabilities have heightened both militarization and volatility. Ultimately, their selective engagement with key normative pillars of the global order reinforces a vision of international politics in which power and strategic self-interest are increasingly accepted as legitimate alternatives to rule-based multilateralism in an era of growing uncertainty.

It is important to recognize that the strategies available to authoritarian middle-powers are likely to be used in different combinations, soft and hard, and that the implications of their foreign policy can only be fully understood by considering the interaction between them. This point is particularly relevant as we move to the next section, as both the justifications for hard foreign policy and the diplomatic and aid policies of such states are intimately bound up with the ideas and ideologies authoritarian middle-powers use to foster legitimacy by engaging in nation-branding.

4 Nation-Branding and the Ideas and Ideologies Used to Foster Legitimacy

An implicit argument underlying the discussion in the previous sections is that non-democratic middle-powers are adept at using political ideas to shape how others see them and hence to shape their position in the world. They are far from alone in this. A broad range of governments from established democracies to authoritarian dictatorships have long understood the importance of discourse as a political tool. Ideas and ideologies assist regimes to sell their performance and enhance their legitimacy at home and abroad. Middle-powers do this as part of a distinctive approach that reflects their size and emphasis on regime survival, however. In turn, this results in a particularly strong emphasis on deploying nation-branding to sanitize their reputation, while forging normative environments more supportive of non-democratic values. As Aydin-Duzgit explains, "discourses are arguably the most potent diplomatic weapon of these powers" (2023: 2320).

This section demonstrates how ideas, images, and symbols are deployed by non-democratic middle-powers, and the considerable resources and time they invest in these projects. In making this argument, we pay significant attention to the way that leaders and ruling parties depict themselves as bearers of alternative political and ideological projects to bolster the image of their country, and draw on populist and/or identity politics to build support. Whether focused on apolitical ideas or more trenchant worldviews such as a return to traditional values, these projects are inherently anti-democratic and shift the global normative landscape, notably by mainstreaming illiberal ideals.

In showing how such public relations campaigns are deployed, and the effects they have on domestic and international audiences, we do not intend to suggest that ideologies are wholly created to serve political ends. In many cases, the public relations that regimes pursue are consistent with the core beliefs of leaders.[24] A classic example is the way that some countries have used their allegiance to Islam to align themselves with other governments and publics. Moreover, such ideational projects will only be effective if they resonate with citizens and external observers, and this is more likely if they are credible. Rather, our aim is to show how certain narratives are intentionally molded and communicated internationally – whether through advertising campaigns, sponsorship deals, or speeches at the United Nations – in pursuit of strategic goals and especially regime endurance.

In doing so, we pay attention both to the ideological frames that are developed and the way that ideas are communicated. As Nic Cheeseman et al. have argued

---

[24] We thank Jonathan Leader Maynard for this point.

(2024), the effectiveness of ideas depends in part on how they are carried – through the media, through channels of information and disinformation – and the extent to which they are institutionalized, for example, in the policy of governments and regional organizations. We begin by discussing different authoritarian nation-branding strategies, before narrowing the focus to address how ideas, ideologies, and identities are used in the service of diffusing non-democratic norms, drawing on a range of examples including Ethiopia and Gulf states.

Controlling Images of the Regime Abroad: Nation-Branding

As Petra Alderman argues (2024: ix), "nation branding is a political act that is integral to state legitimation processes, particularly in the context of authoritarian regimes." In creative hands, it can be a tool of strategic reputation management and reputation building, both domestically and internationally. In terms of domestically focused nation-branding, this is often rooted in the promotion of strategic national myths (Alderman 2024: ix). When projected abroad, this branding makes "achieving foreign policy goals easier and helps marginalise foreign critics. It also makes it tougher for exiles and domestic activists to work together" (Dukalskis 2021b).

The type of branding efforts that authoritarian middle-powers engage in are very different to those of their democratic counterparts, which have largely been centered on promoting liberal-democratic norms. Most notably, authoritarian middle-powers tend to place a greater emphasis on legitimacy gained through performance, service delivery, and the ability to maintain political stability, rather than that gained through the ballot box. In their study of the types of legitimization strategies regimes employ, for example, Von Soest and Grauvogel stress how such regimes emphasize ideologies that highlight the extent to which they deliver for citizens (2017). Such messaging has a twofold benefit. Internationally, it enables governments to claim they are developmental states and hence worthy recipients of foreign assistance. Domestically, it can help to manage dissent and persuade citizens that they are being well served. This is particularly significant given that most non-democratic political systems are competitive-authoritarian states that hold heavily constrained elections, and leaders are well aware that electoral manipulation is easier if it is underpinned by genuine popularity (Cheeseman and Klaas 2024).

When done well, for example by tying nation-branding efforts to the achievement of targets prioritized by Western states such as Sustainable Development Goals, nation-branding efforts of this kind can make states into "beacons" that are seen as models for others to aspire to, enabling governments to garner positive attention abroad and legitimacy at home. Illustrating this, Ethiopia – a borderline middle-power, but the third largest economy in sub-Saharan Africa – successfully marketed its efforts at poverty reduction and economic transformation to foreign partners, both democratic and authoritarian. Under the government of Prime Minister Meles Zenawi, the country was consistently one of the top recipients of foreign aid from the United States and United Kingdom despite repeatedly manipulating elections and abusing human rights (Brown and Fisher 2020). Meles also argued that his regime deserved support because it provided stability in a region marked by civil strife and instability. As Cheeseman and Fisher (2019) have argued, this is a common theme among authoritarian African states, which often emphasize values such as stability, order, and unity because these issues resonate strongly with voters, especially in post-conflict settings.

Authoritarian middle-powers also draw on alternative visions of good government and state performance to bolster domestic legitimacy and cultivate international solidarity, linking local concerns to global narratives. In Africa, for example, the promotion of unity and order resonates particularly powerfully when framed in terms of pan-Africanism and the defense of African values against external intervention. The slogan "African solutions for African problems" has gained traction in countries like Ethiopia and South Africa, as well as among regional elites. Elsewhere, such narratives have invoked economic justice. In Venezuela, successive leaders have framed their authoritarian policies as part of a broader struggle for domestic equality and global socialism, aligning with left-leaning powers like China. Such appeals to anti-imperialism have become potent national brands and ideological glue for international alliances. The critique that the global economic system is rigged against the Global South, for example, has underpinned coalition-building among states like the members of BRICS and ALBA.

There has also been considerable variation in terms of whether authoritarian middle-powers promote more overtly political or a-political brands. While Venezuela represents an excellent example of the former, Gulf States have been exemplars of the latter. Zeinedinne suggests, for example, that "empathetic branding" among Gulf Cooperation Council states has "focused on tourism development, aviation, real estate and international events and exhibitions/conferences, meant to place their countries and capitals ... on the map of the world economy" (2017: 209). This type of branding, based on a more market-oriented image and technical achievements, has the advantage of being less controversial and reducing the risk of pushback from rival powers.

Perhaps the most comprehensive example of such a campaign is recent Emirati nation-branding, complete with a logo, website, and press kit to promote a new vision of the country.[25] This brand centers on the country's purported values of diversity, aspirations of human happiness, hope, and generosity. Rather than selling itself on the basis of its political system, the UAE emphasizes humanistic ideals that serve to "depoliticize" the country's image both offline and online, and hence beyond its borders (Uniacke 2021: 979). Brand analysts have interpreted this change as an attempt to shift the narrative away from older images of a backward-looking rentier monarchical state to that of a modern country and economy with forward-looking leadership (Zeinedinne 2018). While boosting the country's reputation, such narratives also have the potential to "crowd-out, delegitimize and ultimately deter political dissidents" (Uniacke 2021: 979). Seen through this lens, the UAE's branding strategy can be understood as an attempt to take control of a carefully curated dominant image of itself and, in the process, to signal the kinds of criticisms and depictions of the government that it is not willing to tolerate. As Ed Schatz (2009) argues, in this way authoritarian regimes can pre-empt dissent by setting the criteria against which they are willing to be evaluated, and the kind of statements that are likely to result in a coercive backlash.

The diverse approaches set out so far have two things in common. First, they differ profoundly from the moral authority claimed by democratic middle-powers, which was rooted in claims to be legitimate governments promoting universal human rights. Second, they represent a fundamental component of authoritarian states' foreign policy. As alluded to in the previous section, Middle Eastern states such as Saudi Arabia and the UAE have been known to work with major public relations firms, including from the United States and the United Kingdom, both to lobby for better economic deals and to improve their image (Dukalskis 2021a; Sakr 2016).

In Türkiye, such lobbying efforts have gone hand in hand with an expensive campaign that aims to capitalize on the country's 600th anniversary in 2053 to promote what President Erdogan has called the "Türkiye Model" as "the foundation for the country's 2053 vision" (Flouros 2021: 1). As with the UAE, this brand draws on certain aspects of Turkish history, most notably its location as the meeting point between different cultures, to depict the country as "a bridge that connects the East and the West." This vision was chosen precisely because it is inclusive and non-threatening to other states, yet also depicts Türkiye as a critical geopolitical meeting point, both historically and today, linking Europe and the MENA region. A further striking feature of this campaign has been the effort invested to "attract the citizens of the country to assist in forming the brand identity by considering themselves 'as the members of the

---

[25] See https://www.nationbrand.ae/en/.

nation, capable of living, working and innovating together, at the same time adjusting their core cultural values to the necessities of modern life'" (Flouros 2021: 3).

Because a significant portion of this branding work takes place online, it has come to be associated with what is increasingly being called "digital authoritarianism" (Dragu and Lupu 2021) – a range of repressive strategies perpetrated through digital technology, including surveillance and disinformation. In particular, the efforts of authoritarian middle-powers to promote positive images of their regime have often been underpinned by the use of surveillance to identify and silence dissenting voices, and the dissemination of propaganda and false information to gain ground in the global marketplace of ideas. According to Andrew Leber and Alexei Abrahams (2019), for example, Middle Eastern regimes have used social media in recent crises to minimize regime criticism and promote positive images through automated bot accounts. Efforts to ensure the dominance of the desired brand therefore go hand-in-hand with the repression of alternative visions across digital spaces.

The spread of digital authoritarianism has partly been driven by the diffusion of strategies employed by tech-savvy great powers such as China and Russia. Yet as the case of Türkiye demonstrates, authoritarian middle-powers have also adopted their own innovative strategies (Aslan and Yilmaz 2024). These adaptations have resulted in "more subtle, temporary, legal, or plausibly deniable forms of 'next generation' controls, increasing use of surveillance, pro-regime content production, behind-the-scenes pressures, and court cases or legal justifications to alter the online informational environment" (Kerr 2018: 3828). In Türkiye, this has meant an increased focus on online propaganda campaigns while "throttle[ing] traffic or regionally block[ing] access for a limited time during 'crises' instead of issuing complete bans" (Aslan and Yilmaz 2024: 1672), a strategy that has become the preferred mechanism of censorship due to the significant reputational costs generated by complete Internet blackouts.

Authoritarian middle-powers are not the only illiberal actors engaging in nation-branding, but their mid-level status means that they are more reliant on these strategies than great powers, and more likely to avoid the kinds of assertive image projected by countries such as Russia. As a result, their branding strategies tend to avoid stressing power or geopolitical ambitions explicitly. In this respect, the branding of authoritarian-middle powers aims to present them as influential and innovative players operating outside the sphere of great power competition to maintain international relevance while avoiding threatening dominant states. In the process, however, these branding efforts contribute to reframing authoritarianism as modern, competent, and globally engaged. By blurring the normative boundaries between liberal and illiberal actors on the international stage, they make authoritarian middle-powers appear more palatable despite their repressive governance – contributing to the global legitimation of authoritarian practices.

Ideas, Ideologies, and Identities in the Service of Non-Democratic Norms

Image management is not the only way authoritarian middle-powers have used ideas in international relations in the service of regime survival. The ideologies and identities promoted by non-democratic middle-powers also contribute to shifting the norms and practices of multilateral institutions and the governments that comprise them. This includes the promotion of what Cooley calls "counter-norms" that support alternative values to the ones underpinning the liberal rules-based order (2015: 49).

Ideologies are not a new political tool, but their significance has at times been overlooked in IR (Leader Maynard and Haas 2022: 1), and the ideologies of non-democratic regimes have often been dismissed on the basis that they are superficial, devoid of intellectual value, and peripheral to political and global developments. This overlooks the role of ideas, ideologies, and identities in shaping the behavior of governments at home and abroad, as has been emphasized by social constructivist and discursive institutionalist scholarships (Leader Maynard and Haas 2022). In the context of authoritarian middle-powers, there are two main ways that such ideological projects have real-world effects: by shaping the views of domestic publics around the world and by changing perceptions of what is normal and feasible within multilateral spaces.

How this process works is well-illustrated by the two types of ideologies summarily introduced in Section 2. Cultural pluralism, often associated with China, is rooted in the notion that there are no universalistic norms and ideas – including democracy and human rights. Social conservatism, perhaps most frequently identified with President Putin in Russia, is centered on a return to traditional or conservative values about societal and political organization. Taken together, over the last decade these narratives have been used to justify both abusing human rights and rejecting the authority of the international community to intervene globally (Ambrosio 2008; Cottiero and Haggard 2023: 11). China has used its promotion of an ideology of civilizational plurality, for example, to push to have the right to development promoted above first-generation human rights such as the freedom of assembly or expression (Ginsburg 2020; Piccone 2018: 4). President Xi used his speech at the launch of China's Global Civilization Initiative (CGI) in 2023, for example, to advocate for these principles.

A number of authoritarian middle-powers have adopted a similar language and used it for their own purposes. Speaking at the same event, President Nicolas Maduro of Venezuela stated: "[w]e believe the historic moment has come and the time of the people has now arrived. It's time to build a new liberalism that is an alternative to barbaric capitalism, economic hegemony and political blackmail, and against imposing development models on others."[26] Venezuela is not the only authoritarian middle-power to have picked up this intellectual thread. Since its launch, the CGI and the principles it embodies have been recognized in bilateral documents signed by China and a number of other states, including Egypt, Hungary, Pakistan, and the UAE.[27]

One of the main variants of this argument has been a more populist anti-establishment critique of the status quo and of liberal, including liberal internationalist, projects. As we have argued elsewhere, "one of the most notable features ... is the ideological diversity of this range of regimes," from the left-wing populism of Nicaragua's Daniel Ortega to the ring-wing imaginaries of Jair Bolsonaro when he was in power in Brazil or Viktor Orbán in Hungary (Cheeseman 2022: 231). Yet despite this diversity, there is a common theme to most populist discourse, namely that individual leaders, as those who channel the popular will, should be able to make decisions without being stymied by political structures – domestic or international – or the need to compromise. This approach inherently challenges political systems premised on institutional checks and balances, which includes not only democratic political systems at the domestic level but also rules-based decision-making at the international level (Paris 2020).

Populist rhetoric has perhaps been most challenging to human rights in countries where it has gone hand in hand with the rise of social conservatism, and the related re-assertion of patriarchal societies as discussed in Section 2. In practice, this has often meant that women are expected to give up their career ambitions to devote their time to childcare, while LGBTQI+ communities are expected to be less visible – and in some cases are fully criminalized. While Russia has developed this narrative to counter Western norms by arguing that they do not respect key features of Russian tradition (Cooley 2015), some of the most comprehensive use of these ideas have come from Poland and Hungary. In Poland, for example, the right-wing Law and Justice Party (PiS) party promoted policies it believed would be more popular with conservative

---

[26] Both excerpts appear in an event communiqué: https://www.idcpc.org.cn/english/chinainsight/202304/P020230414383512464161.pdf.

[27] As reported by the *People's Daily*, the Chinese Communist Party's official newspaper: https://www.prnewswire.com/apac/news-releases/global-civilization-initiative-conforms-to-trend-meets-demand-of-times-302171872.html.

and religious voters, such as a strong focus on law and order. Prime Minister Mateusz Morawiecki, for example, publicly proclaimed his support for the death penalty and restrictions on women's rights. Though stemming from a different ideological base to China's civilizational plurality, such calls for a return to traditional values are also a fundamental rejection of the idea that there are universal human rights.

As this discussion suggests, the ideological projects of authoritarian states can also be centered on identity politics. To sell their ideas and ideologies abroad, some authoritarian middle-powers have emphasized shared political, ethnic and/or religious values in order to establish a them-versus-us binary designed to foster loyalty at home and solidarity abroad. One of the most extreme variants of this is the revolutionary ideology of the Islamic Republic of Iran, which draws on aspects of Shia Islam and blends them with elements from the 1979 Islamic Revolution, including a belief in self-sufficiency, and a strong anti-Westernism and anti-imperialism. Positioning itself as a champion of Muslims worldwide, the Iranian government uses public statements in support of its allies – and a range of soft power strategies including cultural exchanges, films, and sports diplomacy – to build support for its interventions, including providing financial and military backing for a range of groups such as Hezbollah in Lebanon.

A key element of this program is the activities organized by the Islamic Culture and Relations Organization (ICRO), which operates under the Ministry of Culture and Islamic Guidance. The stated aims of the ICRO are to promote "consolidation of cultural ties of the Islamic Republic of Iran with other nations; [offer] proper presentation of the Iranian culture and civilization; preparing the grounds for unity among Muslims; revival and promotion of Islamic culture and teachings in the world; and information dissemination about the principles and realities of the Islamic Revolution."[28] In this way, identity politics are used to create the ideological glue needed to cement alliances between countries that sometimes have little in common except a set of grievances or enemies, most notably the United States and Israel. The justification of violent strategies, along with the rejection of many international institutions, represents an explicit challenge to a liberal international order.

Other non-democratic middle-powers have also employed religion to ground their ideological appeals, build solidarity between disparate publics, and broadcast power abroad, albeit in less controversial ways. Authoritarian middle-powers such as Saudi Arabia have frequently used Islam as a tool to endear themselves to other states in their region, and to explain their approach

---

[28] As reflected on the organization's website: https://en.icro.ir/.

regarding governance to Muslim peoples abroad and at home (Townshend, 2020). Meanwhile, Indonesia has been described as leveraging "Islamic diplomacy" and a vision of moderate Islam in its efforts to position itself globally (Burton 2021; tho Seeth 2023). Even in states where the regime is not specifically Islamic in its approach to governance, such as Türkiye, a shared Islamic identity has been used to help build support abroad (Ozturk, 2021).

Like all of the ideas and ideologies described in this section, this focus on religion serves twin international and domestic purposes. On the one hand, it enables states to rally support abroad by differentiating their political system and cultural values from those of their Western counterparts. On the other hand, it reinforces the regime's appeal to their own citizens, with whom the identity resonates, which often includes the more conservative segments of society that are the natural allies of illiberal regimes.

The Impact of Authoritarian Ideas

Nation-branding has a significant impact on how countries are perceived globally. There is considerable evidence that the efforts of middle-powers can cut through, despite the amount of media time and attention given to superpowers such as China and Russia. One reason for this is that less wealthy countries looking for positive examples often conclude that large and industrialized economies such as China are unsuitable role models. Success stories that are closer to home may appear to be more feasible to pursue where the design of political models is concerned. Just as non-democratic middle-powers have drawn lessons from the strategic repertoires of great powers, their deployment of nation-branding and ideational tools is now shaping the practices of other states, thereby advancing and legitimizing notions that diverge from the liberal post-War international order.

There is extensive scholarship showing how the global transfer of ideas from authoritarian middle-powers is shaping the political goals and development policies of middle- and small powers. The literature on policy transfer and emulation has consistently demonstrated that African states are not simply following the Chinese model but often identify with Asian exemplars such as Singapore, which they consider to be closer to their economic context and level of development. Kenya's Vision 2030, which was developed following the election of the NaRC government in 2002, for example, was deeply inspired both in content and name by Malaysia's Vision 2020. The same is true of Ethiopia's "growth and stimulation plan" that was developed to guide economic growth between 2010 and 2015. Put differently, the very size of authoritarian and autocratizing middle-powers means they are often seen to be more logical models to imitate than great powers, giving them outsized influence on the world stage. This has meant they play an important role in the transfer of ideas regarding how to undermine critical voices, such as the anti-NGO legislation that has been adopted by an increasing number of states, contributing to a decline in the number of transnational human rights organizations (Fransen and Dupuy 2024).

It is difficult to assess precisely how much impact authoritarian middle-powers' branding and ideologies have had on global attitudes towards the value of democracy, support for illiberal alternatives, and the liberal international order. For example, dissatisfaction with democracy around the world is rooted in a number of different factors, including criticism of the way civilian government are performing. It is striking, however, that public criticism of democracy is rising (Foa et al. 2022: 9) at a time when China has been seen to be a more trusted partner for citizens in Africa than either the United States or the European Union (Afrobarometer 2025), and World Values Survey data records a decline "in public support for "liberalism" and a "worrying drop" in the proportion of citizens saying that "democracy is important.""[29] What is certain is that alternative illiberal narratives are increasingly being promoted internationally – and with considerable success. In a recent survey of pro-democracy and authoritarian messaging globally, the Metropolitan Group found that narratives promoting authoritarianism far outnumbered their democratic counterparts and were often more effective (2025: 14–15). While authoritarian middle-powers have not always led this charge, they have been instrumental in amplifying it.

One reason that authoritarian middle-powers have been such avid users of nation-branding and pro-authoritarian narratives is that they have been shown to have strong benefits at home. A private firm conducting a survey of Saudis' opinion on the country's Vision 2030 – a key nation-branding tool – found overall support for the government's new approach.[30] In a region that was shaken by the Arab Spring uprisings not so long ago, the UAE's rebranding efforts also seem to be paying off. A poll commissioned by the Washington Institute suggests that while not "every policy has universal approval, most Emiratis reject the idea of mass protests against the government – though this was by no means the prevailing attitude just two years before" (Cleveland 2022). The same poll also suggested that Emiratis increasingly see China and Russia as viable alternatives to the United States, a historical backer of the UAE.

---

[29] https://reason.com/2022/12/14/the-world-is-still-getting-less-free-a-distressing-number-of-people-think-thats-fine/
[30] https://www.serco.com/me/me-perspectives-content/tl-si-public-opinion-supports-the-pace-of-change-in-ksa.

Frustrations with the liberal rules-based order also stem from its own inherent contradictions, including the highly unequal power distribution it has reinforced between states, which authoritarian states have proved adept at harnessing for their own purposes. While this process has been led by global powers, it has also been creatively taken on and advanced by a range of middle-powers, many of which have considerable influence in their region, as Türkiye and the UAE demonstrate. There can be no doubt that the constant challenging of democratic norms and values on the international stage by authoritarian middle-powers' counternormative efforts has contributed to cleanse the image of authoritarian regimes who promote alternative political visions, and more broadly to the weakening of democracy's "brand."

It has also contributed to delegitimizing the notions of universalism and even "collectivism" at the core of the global order. In some respects, this has been a welcome and necessary development, for example the challenging of colonial legacies and the tendency to marginalize voices from the Global South. Yet there is a darker side to this trend: it is also legitimizing the rule of repressive governments that are seeking to build a more authoritarian world.

Conclusion: Toward a New Research Agenda on Authoritarian Middle-Powers

Explanations of the growing challenges to the post-War liberal international order and the global democratic recession of the last two decades have tended to identify China and Russia as the predominant drivers of these trends. Following recent events in the United States, this focus is likely to extend to the role played by the Trump administration. This focus on great and superpowers is understandable, but overlooks the role played by a growing number of influential middle-powers. As this Element has shown, countries such as Iran, Türkiye, and Venezuela are not simply pawns of China and Russia. Instead, they operate with their own agency, pursuing a distinctive form of international relations shaped by their global status and domestic politics that is designed in large part to meet domestic political concerns.

Despite this, IR and comparative politics have largely failed to study authoritarian and autocratizing middle-powers as a category and have paid little attention to how they impact global politics. While traditional middle-power theory has addressed how the size and capacity of a state impact foreign policy, it has largely focused on democratic states and cannot fully capture the behavior of non-democratic actors on the international scene. The different approach of authoritarian middle-powers and the shifting international context in which they operate necessitate revising our theoretical understanding of middle-powers. This Element has demonstrated how the quest for regime survival of these states, along with their mid-level status, has shaped their international relations in ways that have created a more inhospitable international environment for the promotion of democratic norms.

Our first cut at reformulating middle-power theory suggests that, lacking the capacity and might of great powers, authoritarian middle-powers tend to view international relations and foreign policy as a way to enhance their domestic survival. They are pragmatic when engaging abroad, pursuing strategies likely to render them more secure and popular at home. This makes their foreign policy self-serving, short-termist, and at times even apparently contradictory. It is largely driven by the desire to form international marriages of convenience in order to better target political opponents and generate an international environment more accommodating of illiberal policies and practices. In most cases, this manifests in the simultaneous use of hard and soft power and in forms of omnibalancing.

Authoritarian middle-powers have remained actively engaged in global arenas, including multilateral institutions, using these spaces to hedge and maintain ties with a broad range of allies. This has not been driven by a commitment to liberal norms but rather by a desire to maintain relations with a wide range of allies and to reshape these institutions from within. More specifically, undemocratic mid-ranking states have sought to turn these organizations into environments that protect or advance their political survival, diluting their commitment to democracy and human rights. Regionally and bilaterally, their influence has often been deeper. In both formal and informal regional forums – many of which they have contributed to create or have transformed – authoritarian middle-powers promote authoritarian norms and practices through coordination, mutual support, while targeting political opponents of allied regimes. These forums have also become hubs of authoritarian learning and for the diffusion of new strategies, including citizen surveillance and civil society repression.

Even more disruptive has been authoritarian middle-powers' willingness to deploy hard power. States such as UAE and Türkiye routinely use military force, from regional coercion to "drone diplomacy" and expanded defense cooperation. These efforts have militarized fellow authoritarian states and pushed international red lines, increasing risks of instability and conflict. Meanwhile, the pursuit of regional dominance – as seen in Iran and Saudi Arabia – has further destabilized surrounding areas, especially where rival authoritarian middle-powers compete. In regions where China and Russia are less dominant, such as parts of the Middle East, Latin America, and the Near East, authoritarian middle-powers are shaping political developments by undermining rivals and drawing others into their authoritarian orbit. In this respect, though not in others, their tactics resemble those of authoritarian great powers more than of democratic counterparts. In turn, this feature of their behavior reveals a core inconsistency: while promoting sovereignty as a foundational principle of international relations, these regimes frequently violate it themselves.

Regional politics is also where the foreign policy of authoritarian middle-powers has been most contradictory and destabilizing. The quest for regional dominance, for example, can cut against the strategy of hedging and alliance formation, resulting in lost international friends and generating new challenges to the retention of power. Iran is an example of the costs that an aggressive approach to international relations can generate, having been not only shunned but also sanctioned by other powers. Yet it is also an example that highlights the creativity and flexibility of authoritarian middle-powers, as the Iranian government has pivoted to form new "anti-sanctions" alliances with countries as far afield as Venezuela and the new junta in Niger. During a visit of Niger's new prime minister to Tehran, for example Iran's first prime minister was quoted as saying his country would support Niger, in the face of "cruel sanctions which are imposed by the domination system."[31] In addition to fueling regional instability, military interventions and support for armed actors in neighboring conflicts has helped to normalize the perception that international rules are negotiable. While great powers like Russia have led the charge in dismantling key norms through high-profile actions such as in Ukraine, it is often authoritarian middle-powers that lend regional legitimacy to these trends.

At the same time, authoritarian middle-powers have deployed thematic, cultural, and public diplomacy through nation-branding efforts and soft power projection to counterbalance their more aggressive strategies, while also challenging liberal ideals. Rather than promoting universalist values such as human rights or democratic participation, they present themselves as pragmatic, stable, and economically competent – qualities that resonate in many parts of the Global South. The cumulative effect of these efforts is the normalization of illiberal governance as legitimate and effective, particularly in regions where democratic institutions remain fragile. In discrediting universalist liberal norms, these actors open space for repressive regimes to reframe themselves not as aberrations but as legitimate alternatives. This is therefore another way in which authoritarian middle-powers have brought about a world more tolerant of autocratic behaviors, challenging the international promotion of democracy and human rights, while seeking to promote alternative norms more conducive to their form of politics, such as the right to sovereignty.

Although the depiction of undemocratic political systems and practices as innocuous and palatable has largely been pursued for self-serving domestic ends, it nonetheless poses a real threat to democratic and liberal internationalist norms – as illustrated by the growing popularity of some of these alternative ideologies, including among citizens of democratic countries. When combined with the impact of authoritarian great powers on world politics, the broader implications of these trends are profound, contributing to a form of international politics where transactionalism displaces efforts to provide global collective goods, and where global, regional, and bilateral frameworks are increasingly reoriented to serve narrow regime objectives rather than shared governance principles.

In addition, the hollowing out of multilateral institutions risks leaving them devoid of the collective will and norms to tackle pressing global challenges. Multilateralism has never been a perfect tool to manage global security challenges, as the critics of the UN have regularly pointed out. Yet the efforts of

---

[31] https://www.voanews.com/a/iran-says-it-is-willing-to-help-niger-overcome-sanctions/7455787.html.

democratic middle-powers in an internationalist epoch did enable the emergence of new collective institutions that played a role in entrenching human rights and liberal norms, such as the creation of the International Criminal Court. There is likely to be less potential for multilateral scrutiny of domestic practices moving forwards, given the effective mobilization of authoritarian middle- and great powers in favour of norms of sovereignty and non-interference. The same is true for collaborative international responses to common challenges such as climate change. In this way, authoritarian middle-powers are actively contributing to a more conflict-prone world in which collective problem-solving becomes even rarer.

Middle-Power Agency

Countries such as Azerbaijan and Egypt are not doing this alone, of course. They often form wider alliances with stronger states such as China and Russia, for example within the UN General Assembly and Human Rights Council. But as this Element has revealed, it is a mistake to treat authoritarian middle-powers as mere proxies of superpowers. While the actions of authoritarian middle-powers may enable China and Russia to pursue some of their core goals, they consistently exert their own agency. Governments in countries such as Iran, Türkiye, and Venezuela pursue their own goals for their own reasons, and at times have acted in ways that did not advance the interests of authoritarian great powers. Moreover, the tendency of authoritarian middle-powers to hedge means that they are often reluctant to align too closely to either China or Russia, especially when doing so would make them a potential enemy of democratic great powers.

This is a critical point, because it is only when the short-termist and hedging nature of middle-powers is foregrounded that it becomes clear that the future is unlikely to see the emergence of a stable and united authoritarian power bloc on the world stage. Instead, the pragmatic nature of authoritarian middle-powers' foreign policy means that coalition-building will continue to go hand in hand with competition, uncertainty and instability. This is evidenced by the recent conflicts and fallouts between states in the Middle East, including the war in Yemen involving Iran and Saudi Arabia. It is also demonstrated by the way that the UAE's involvement in Sudan has contributed to a deepening of the civil war and by the rollercoaster of international relations between Venezuela and Brazil in recent years – including the recent deployment of Brazilian troops to the Venezuelan border in response to Venezuela's territorial claim over the Essequibo region, understood by most governments to belong to Guyana.

These constant tensions and episodic disruptions reveal the flaw in analyses that predict a single and coherent movement toward a global authoritarian future driven by China and Russia. Instead, a careful study of authoritarian middle-powers suggests the emergence of a new phase of international relations characterized at least in part by idiosyncratic patterns of collaboration and conflict driven by domestic concerns, most notably regime survival. Put another way, the future may be authoritarian, but this process is likely to be a far more complex and unpredictable than narratives of a coordinated and coherent assault on the liberal international order suggest.

Additional research is therefore needed into the international relations of authoritarian middle-powers and the impact they will have on world politics as the post-War liberal epoch increasingly gives way to a more undemocratic and multipolar era. Many aspects of middle-power behavior remain poorly understood. One valuable research agenda would focus on how these states – and their governments – communicate and coordinate with one another, and the balance between formal and informal approaches in this process. The way that authoritarian middle-powers and great powers engage is also understudied, especially given the implicit but misleading tendency to assume that authoritarian middle-powers either follow or emulate the strategies of larger authoritarian actors globally. A better understanding of these relations is key given the potential significance of these relationships to any future struggles between East and West, or North and South.

There is also more work to be done with regard to the likely impact of authoritarian middle-powers on global politics. We have summarized some of these impacts as they manifest today, while noting the challenges involved in doing so, especially in a limited number of words. If current trends continue and these states become more numerous – and especially if the United States itself continues to undermine global norms and to challenge existing democracy and human rights standards – we may find ourselves in a new era in which global events are increasingly driven by authoritarian middle-power behavior, as in the 1930s. If so, the greater emboldening of such regimes may require a further evolution in the theoretical framework developed here, reminding us once again that foreign policy is a function of the interaction between domestic politics and international context.

Abbreviations

ALBA	Bolivarian Alliance for the People of our America
CGI	Global Civilization Initiative
DAC	Development Assistance Committee
DIA	Defense Intelligence Agency
GDP	Gross Domestic Product
GNP	Gross National Product
ICRO	Islamic Culture and Relations Organization
IR	International Relations
LMG	Like-Minded Group
NATO	North Atlantic Treaty Organization
NGOs	Non-Governmental Organizations
OTS	Organization of Turkic States
PKK	Kurdistan Workers Party
RSF	Rapid Support Forces
SAF	Sudanese Armed Forces
SIPRI	Stockholm International Peace Research Institute
SLTD	Stolen and Lost Travel Document
TITR	Trans-Caspian International Transport Route
UAE	United Arab Emirates
UN	United Nations
UNHRC	United Nations Human Rights Council

References

Abbondanza, Gabriele, and Thomas Stow Wilkins, eds. 2022. *Awkward Powers: Escaping Traditional Great and Middle Power Theory*, Singapore, Palgrave MacMillan.

Abrams, Elliott. 2022. "The new cold war," Council on Foreign Relations, www.cfr.org/blog/new-cold-war-0.

Afrobarometer, 2025, "R10 2024/2025 data", Afrobarometer, https://www.afrobarometer.org/online-data-analysis/.

Akpinar, Pinar. 2015. "Mediation as a foreign policy tool in the Arab Spring: Turkey, Qatar and Iran," *Journal of Balkan and Near Eastern Studies* 17(3), 252–268.

Alderman, Petra. 2024. *Branding Authoritarian Nations: Political Legitimation and Strategic National Myths in Military-Ruled Thailand*, London, Routledge.

Alhussain, Eman. 2022. "Saudi Arabia's branding strategy," The Arab Gulf State Institute in Washington, June 9, https://agsiw.org/wp-content/uploads/2022/06/Alhussein_Soft-power-1.pdf.

Alpan, Başak, and Ahmet Erdi Öztürk. 2022. "Turkish foreign policy in the Balkans amidst 'soft power' and 'de-Europeanisation'," *Southeast European and Black Sea Studies* 22(1), 45–63.

Ambrosio, Thomas. 2008. "Catching the 'Shanghai spirit': How the Shanghai Cooperation Organization promotes authoritarian norms in Central Asia," *Europe-Asia Studies* 60(8), 1321–1344.

Ashford, Emma, and Evan Cooper. 2023. "Yes, the world is multipolar," Foreign Policy, October 5, https://foreignpolicy.com/2023/10/05/usa-china-multipolar-bipolar-unipolar/.

Aslan, Mesut, and Gözde Yilmaz. 2024. "Diffusion of digital authoritarianism? Censorship, surveillance and beyond in Türkiye," *Third World Quarterly* 45(10), 1663–1681.

Aydin, Umut. 2021. "Emerging middle powers and the liberal international order," International Affairs 97(5), 1377–1394.

Aydin-Düzgit, Senem. 2023. "Authoritarian middle powers and the liberal order: Turkey's contestation of the EU," International Affairs 99(6), 2319–2337.

Aydın-Düzgit, Senem, Mustafa Kutlay, and E. Fuat Keyman. 2025. "Strategic autonomy in Turkish foreign policy in an age of multipolarity: lineages and contradictions of an idea," International Politics, https://link.springer.com/article/10.1057/s41311-024-00638-w#citeas.

Barker, Jennie. 2024. "The Changing Geopolitical Landscape for Support for Democracy." Paper presented at the American Political Science Association Annual Convention, Philadelphia, United States, 6 September.

Baser, Bahar, and Ahmet Erdi Ozturk. 2020. "Positive and negative diaspora governance in context: From public diplomacy to transnational authoritarianism," *Middle East Critique* 29(3), 319–334.

Bekkevold, Jo Inge. 2023. "No, the world is not multipolar," Foreign Policy, September 22, https://foreignpolicy.com/2023/09/22/multipolar-world-bipolar-power-geopolitics-business-strategy-china-united-states-india/.

Bennis, Amine. 2020. "Middle power diplomacy: From state to thematic diplomacy," Global Policy Opinion, April 6, www.globalpolicyjournal.com/blog/06/04/2020/middle-power-diplomacy-state-thematic-diplomacy.

Bettiza, Gregorio, and David Lewis. 2020. "Authoritarian powers and norm contestation in the liberal international order: Theorizing the power politics of ideas and identity," *Journal of Global Security Studies* 5(4), 559–577.

Böcü, Gözde, and Bahar Baser. 2024. "Transnational mobilization of future generations by non-democratic home states: Turkey's diaspora youth between empowerment and co-optation," *Ethnopolitics* 23(1), 34–58.

Brown, Stephen, and Jonathan Fisher. 2020. "Aid donors, democracy and the developmental state in Ethiopia," *Democratization* 27(2), 185–203.

BTI. 2024a. *Transformation Index BTI 2024*, Berlin, BTI.

BTI. 2024b. "Country report: Nicaragua," Berlin, https://bti-project.org/fileadmin/api/content/en/downloads/reports/country_report_2024_NIC.pdf.

Bueno De Mesquita, Bruce, Alastair Smith, Randolph M. Siverson, and James D. Morrow. 2005. *The Logic of Political Survival*, Cambridge: MIT Press.

Burton, Guy. 2021. "Middle power behavior under multipolarity: Indonesia and Malaysia in the Middle East since the Arab uprisings," *Asian Politics & Policy* 13(2), 228–247.

Chapnick, Adam. 2000. "The Canadian middle power myth," *International Journal* 55(2), 188–206.

Cheeseman, Nic. 2022. "Populism across borders: How foreign leaders encourage and sustain populists abroad," in Tendai Biti, Nic Cheeseman, Christopher Clapham, et al., eds., In the Name of the People: How Populism is Rewiring the World, Johannesburg, Picador Africa, 290–314.

Cheeseman, Nic, and Marie-Eve Desrosiers. 2023. *"How (Not) To Engage with Authoritarian States*," Westminster Foundation for Democracy, London, February.

Cheeseman, Nic, Marie-Eve Desrosiers, Licia Cianetti, and Manoel Gehrke. 2024a. "How to strengthen democratic resilience: Five lessons for democratic renewal," European Democracy Hub, December, https://epd.eu/news-publications/how-to-strengthen-democratic-resilience-five-lessons-for-democratic-renewal/.

Cheeseman, Nic, and Jonathan Fisher. 2019. *Authoritarian Africa: Repression, Resistance, and the Power of Ideas*, Oxford, Oxford University Press.

Cheeseman, Nic, and Brian Klass. 2024. *How to Rig an Election*, 2nd ed., New Haven, Yale University Press.

Cheeseman, Nic, Fisher, Jonathan, Mwambari, David. 2025. Authoritarianism in Sub-Saharan Africa. In Anne M. Wolfe (ed.) The Oxford Handbook of Authoritarian Politics. Oxford, Oxford University Press.

Christensen, J. (2021). The morality of substitution intervention: The case of Yemen. Politics, 43(3), 315–329.

Christensen, James. 2023. "The morality of substitution intervention: The case of Yemen," *Politics*, 43(3), 315–329.

Cleveland, Catherine. 2022. "New UAE poll shows nuance on domestic issues; growing public uncertainty over U.S. relations; split views of Iran & Israel," Fikra Forum, December 20, www.washingtoninstitute.org/policy-analysis/new-uae-poll-shows-nuance-domestic-issues-growing-public-uncertainty-over-us.

Cooley, Alexander. 2015. "Authoritarianism goes global: Countering democratic norms," *Journal of Democracy* 26(3), 49–63.

Cooper, Andrew F., ed. 1997. *Niche Diplomacy: Middle Powers after the Cold War*, London: Macmillan.

Cooper, Andrew F. 2018. "Entrepreneurial states versus middle powers: Distinct or intertwined frameworks?" *International Journal* 73(4), 596–608.

Cooper, Andrew F., and Daniel Flemes. 2013. "Foreign policy strategies of emerging powers in a multipolar world: An introductory essay," *Third World Quarterly* 34(6), 943–962.

Cooper, Andrew F., Richard A. Higgott, and Kim R. Nossal. 1993. *Relocating Middle Powers: Australia and Canada in a Changing World Order*, Vancouver, UBC Press.

Cooper, Andrew, and Emel Dal Parlar. 2016. "Positioning the third wave of middle power diplomacy: Institutional elevation, practice limitations," *International Journal* 71, 516–528.

Cooper, David A. 2011. "Challenging contemporary notions of middle-power influence: Implications of the proliferation security initiative for 'middle-power theory'," *Foreign Policy Analysis* 7(3), 317–336.

Cottiero, Christina, and Stephan Haggard. 2023. "Stabilizing authoritarian rule: The role of international organizations," *International Studies Quarterly*, advanced online.

David, James W. 2023. "Better than a bet: Good reasons for behavioral and rational choice assumptions in IR," *European Journal of International Relations* 29(2), 476–500.

de Mesquita, Bruce B., and Randolph M. Siverson. 1995. "War and the survival of political leaders: A comparative study of regime types and political accountability," *American Political Science Review* 89(4), 841–855.

de Mesquita, Bruce B., and Alastair Smith. 2011. *The Dictator's Handbook: Why Bad Behavior Is Almost Always Good Politics*, New York, Public Affairs.

DIA, "Seized At Sea: Iranian Weapons Smuggled to the Houthis", 30 April 2024, online:https://www.dia.mil/Portals/110/Documents/News/Military_Power_Publications/Seized_at_Sea.pdf.

Ding, Long. 2024. "The evolving roles of the gulf states in the horn of Africa," *Asian Journal of Middle Eastern and Islamic Studies* 18(1), 1–14.

Dipama, Samiratou, and Emel Parlar. 2023. "Assessing Turkey-Africa engagements," APRI Policy Brief 2/2023, Berlin.

Doğangün, Gokten. 2020. "Gender climate in authoritarian politics: A comparative study of Russia and Turkey," *Politics & Gender* 16(1), 258–284.

Dragu, Tiberiu, and Yonatan Lupu. 2021. "Digital authoritarianism and the future of human rights," *International Organization* 75(4), 991–1017.

Dukalskis, Alexander. 2021a. *Making the World Safe for Dictatorship*, Oxford, Oxford University Press.

Dukalskis, Alexander. 2021b. "How authoritarian rulers manage their international image." The Conversation, https://theconversation.com/how-authoritarian-rulers-manage-their-international-image-166778.

Dukalskis, Alexander, Saipira Furstenberg, Yana Gorokhovskaia, et al. 2022. "Transnational repression: Data advances, comparisons, and challenges," *Political Research Exchange* 4(1), 1–17.

Edström, Håkan, and Jacob Westberg. 2020. "The defense strategies of middle powers: Competing for security, influence and status in an era of unipolar demise," *Comparative Strategy* 39(2), 171–190.

Efstathopoulos, Charalampos. 2021. "Southern middle powers and the liberal international order: The options for Brazil and South Africa," *International Journal* 76(3), 384–403.

Emmons, Cassandra V. 2020. "International organizations: Enablers or impediments for authoritarian international law?" *AJIL Unbound* 114, 226–231.

Farouk, Yasmine. 2020. "Saudi Arabia: Aid as a primary foreign policy tool," Carnegie Endowment for Peace, https://carnegieendowment.org/2020/06/09/saudi-arabia-aid-as-primary-foreign-policy-tool-pub-82003.

References

Fisher, Jonathan. 2023. "Authoritarian futures: (In)Security and futurocratic governance in Africa and beyond," ECAS, Cologne, Germany, May 30.

Flemes, Daniel. 2007. "Emerging middle powers' soft balancing strategy: State and perspectives of the IBSA dialogue forum," GIGA, Paper 57, August, https://edoc.vifapol.de/opus/volltexte/2009/1617/pdf/wp57flemes.pdf.

Flouros, Floros. 2021. "Turkey's nation branding for the 2050s: Challenges and opportunities," Handbook of Research on Future Policies and Strategies for Nation Branding, Hershey, IGI Global.

Foa, Roberto Stefan, Klassen, Andrew, Slade, Michael, Rand, Alex. and Collins, Rebecca. 2020. *The Global Satisfaction with Democracy Report 2020*, Cambridge, Centre for the Future of Democracy.

Fradkin, Hillel, and Lewis Libby. 2013. "Erdogan's grand vision: Rise and decline," *World Affairs* 175(6), 41–50.

Fransen, Luc, and Kendra E. Dupuy. 2024. "Death by law: Restrictive regulations and INGO numbers," *International Journal of Politics, Culture, and Society* 37, 433–445.

Freedom House 2021a. "Saudi Arabia: Transnational repression origin country case study," https://freedomhouse.org/report/transnational-repression/saudi-arabia.

Freedom House 2021b. "Turkey: Transnational repression origin country case study," https://freedomhouse.org/report/transnational-repression/turkey.

Freedom House 2022. "The global expansion of authoritarian rule," Freedom House, https://freedomhouse.org/report/freedom-world/2022/global-expansion-authoritarian-rule.

Fruh, Kyle, Alfred Archer, and Jake Wojtowicz. 2023. "Sportswashing: Complicity and corruption," *Sport, Ethics and Philosophy* 17(1), 101–118.

Fukuyama, Francis. 1992. *The End of History and the Last Man*, New York, Free Press.

Gallarotti, Giulio, and Isam Yahia Al-Filali. 2014. "Saudi Arabia's soft power," *International Studies* 49(3–4), 233–261.

Geddes, Barbara, Joseph Wright, and Erica Frantz. 2014. "Autocratic breakdown and regime transitions: A new data set," *Perspectives on Politics* 12(2), 313–331.

Gehrke, Laurenz. 2020. "Polish PM defends new abortion law as women take to streets," Politico, October 27, www.politico.eu/article/polish-pm-defends-new-abortion-law-as-protests-continue/.

Gerschewski, Johannes. 2023. *The Two Logic of Autocratic Rule*, Cambridge, Cambridge University Press.

Ginsburg, Tom. 2020. "How authoritarians use international law," *Journal of Democracy* 31(4), 44–58.

Glazebrook, George de T. (1947). "The middle powers in the United Nations system," *International Organization* 1(2), 307–315.

Grix, Jonathan, Adam Dinsmore, and Paul Michael Brannagan. 2023. "Unpacking the politics of 'sportswashing': It takes two to tango," *Politics*, https://journals.sagepub.com/doi/epub/10.1177/02633957231207387.

Grzywacz, Anna. 2024. *Paper presented at the BISA 2024 Conference, British International Studies Association*, Birmingham, United Kingdom.

Grzywacz, Anna, and Marcin Florian Gawrycki. 2021. "The authoritarian turn of middle powers: Changes in narratives and engagement," *Third World Quarterly* 42(11), 2629–2650.

Gurol, Julia, Alke Jenss, Fabricio Rodríguez, Benjamin Scheutze, Cita Wetterich. 2023. "Authoritarian power and contestation beyond the state," Globalizations, advance online.

Hall, Stephen G. F. 2023. "The role of regional organisations in authoritarian learning," in *The Authoritarian International: Tracing How Authoritarian Regimes Learn in the Post-Soviet Space*, Cambridge, Cambridge University Press, 127–143.

Haqqani, Husain, and Narayanappa Janardhan. 2023. "The minilateral era," Foreign Policy, January 10. https://foreignpolicy.com/2023/01/10/minilateral-diplomacy-middle-power-india-israel-uae/.

Heibach, Jens. 2021. "Public diplomacy and regional leadership struggles: The case of Saudi Arabia," International Politics, https://link.springer.com/article/10.1057/s41311-021-00310-7#citeas.

Holbraad, Carsten. 1984. *Middle Powers in International Politics*, London, MacMillan.

Huijgh, Ellen. 2017. "Indonesia's 'intermestic' public diplomacy: Features and future," *Politics & Policy* 45(5), 762–792.

Human Rights Watch. 2018. "Strengthening the UN human rights council from the ground up," www.hrw.org/news/2018/04/23/strengthening-un-human-rights-council-ground.

Human Rights Watch. 2023. "Azerbaijan: Events of 2023," www.hrw.org/world-report/2024/country-chapters/azerbaijan#:~:text=Long%2Dterm%20human%20rights%20concerns,and%20places%20of%20detention%20persisted.

Humire, Joseph M. 2020. "The Maduro-Hezbollah nexus: How Iran-backed networks prop up the Venezuelan regime," Atlantic Council Latin America Center, www.atlanticcouncil.org/wp-content/uploads/2020/10/The-Maduro-Hezbollah-Nexus-How-Iran-backed-Networks-Prop-up-the-Venezuelan-Regime.pdf.

Iddon, Paul. 2023. "Russia-Iran arms deal could be a win-win for Moscow and Tehran," Forbes, November 29, www.forbes.com/sites/pauliddon/2023/11/28/russia-iran-arms-deal-could-be-a-win-win-for-moscow-and-tehran/.

Ikenberry, G. John. 2016. "Between the eagle and the dragon: America, China, and middle state strategies in East Asia," *Political Science Quarterly* 131(1), 9–43.

Inboden, Rana Siu. 2019. "Authoritarian states: Blocking civil society participation in the United Nations," Robert Strauss Center for International Security and Law, Austin, University of Texas at Austin, www.strausscenter.org/wp-content/uploads/strauss/18-19/RSInbodenAuthoritarianStates.pdf.

International Crisis Group. 2023. "Türkiye's growing drone exports," December 20, www.crisisgroup.org/sites/default/files/2024-02/turkey-drones-6ii2024.pdf.

Jervis, Robert. 1976. *Perception and Misperception in International Politics*, Princeton, Princeton University Press.

Jordaan, Eduard. 2003. "The concept of a middle power in international relations: Distinguishing between emerging and traditional middle powers," *South African Journal of Political Science* 30(1), 165–181.

Kerr, Jaclyn A. 2018. "Information, security, and authoritarian stability: Internet policy diffusion and coordination in the former soviet region," *International Journal of Communication* 12(1), 3814–3834.

King, Samuel, and Inés Pousadela. 2025. "Strengthening the UN Human Rights Council: Pathways to enhanced credibility and effectiveness," Ensured, www.ensuredeurope.eu/publications/strengthening-the-un-human-rights-council.

Kneuer, Marianne, Thomas Demmelhuber, Raphael Peresson, and Tobias Zumbrägel. 2019. "Playing the regional card: Why and how authoritarian gravity centres exploit regional organisations," *Third World Quarterly*, 40(3), 451–470.

Krzymowski, Adam. 2022. "Role and significance of the United Arab Emirates foreign aid for its soft power strategy and sustainable development goals," *Social Sciences* 11(2), 48–66.

Kutlay, Mustafa. 2025. "Turkey's middle-power Dilemma: The overlooked costs of a transnational foreign policy," Foreign Affairs, May 15, www.foreignaffairs.com/turkey/turkeys-middle-power-dilemma.

Kutlay, Mustafa, and Ziya Öniş. 2021. "Understanding oscillations in Turkish foreign policy: Pathways to unusual middle power activism," *Third World Quarterly* 42(12), 3051–3069.

LaFleur, Jennifer. 2009. "Adding it up: The top players in foreign agent lobbying," ProPublica, August 18, www.propublica.org/article/adding-it-up-the-top-players-in-foreign-agent-lobbying-718.

Leader Maynard, Jonathan, and Mark L. Haas. Eds. 2022. *The Routledge Handbook of Ideology and International Relations*, London, Routledge.

Leber, Andrew, and Alexei Abrahams. 2019. "A storm of tweets: Social media manipulation during the Gulf Crisis," *Review of Middle East Studies* 53(2), 241–258.

Leira, Halvard. 2019. "The emergence of foreign policy," *International Studies Quarterly* 63(1), 187–198.

Lemon, Edward. 2019. "Weaponizing Interpol," *Journal of Democracy* 30(2), 15–29.

Levitsky, Steven et Lucan Way. 2010. *Competitive Authoritarianism: Hybrid Regimes after the Cold War*, Cambridge, Cambridge University Press.

Levy, Ido. 2024. "Emirati military support is making a difference in Somalia," Washington Institute for near East Policy, March 18, www.washingtoninstitute.org/policy-analysis/emirati-military-support-making-difference-somalia.

Libman, Alexander, and Anastassia V. Obydenkova. 2018. "Understanding authoritarian regionalism," *Journal of Democracy* 29(4), 151–165.

Lopez, C. Todd. 2024. "Iran gives Russia short-range missiles, while U.S., partners expect to keep bolstering Ukrainian air defense," U.S. Department of Defense, September 10, www.defense.gov/News/News-Stories/Article/Article/3901774/iran-gives-russia-short-range-missiles-while-us-partners-expect-to-keep-bolster/.

Mahjoub, Husam. 2024. "It's an open secret: The UAE is fuelling Sudan's war – and there'll be no peace until we call it out," The Guardian, May 24, www.theguardian.com/commentisfree/article/2024/may/24/uae-sudan-war-peace-emirates-uk-us-officials.

Mansfield, Edward D., and John C. Pevehouse. 2006. "Democratization and international organizations," *International Organization* 60(1), 137–167.

Mattes, Michaela, and Mariana Rodriguez. 2014. "Autocracies and international cooperation," *International Studies Quarterly* 58, 527–538.

McLoughlin, Stephen, Jess Gifkins, and Alex J. Bellamy. (2023). "The evolution of mass atrocity early warning in the UN Secretariat: Fit for purpose?" *International Peacekeeping* 30(4), 477–505.

Mearsheimer, John J., and Sebastian Rosato. 2023. *How States Think: The Rationality of Foreign Policy*, New Haven, Yale University Press.

Mearsheimer, John J., and Sebastian Rosato. 2024. "Essence of decision-making," Foreign Affairs January-February.

Metropolitan Group. 2025. "A new narrative to promote democracy in the United States: A findings and recommendations report," May, www.metgroup.com/wp-content/uploads/2025/06/MG-US-Democracy-Narratives-Report_FINAL_June-18-2025.pdf.

Miller, Rory, and Sarah Cardaun. 2020. "Multinational security coalitions and the limits of middle power activism in the Middle East: The Saudi case," *International Affairs* 96(6), 1509–1525.

Nagy, Stephen, and Jonathan Ping. 2023. "The end of the normative middle power ship," Australian Outlook, Australian Institute of International Affairs, March 14, www.internationalaffairs.org.au/australianoutlook/the-end-of-the-normative-middle-power-ship/.

Nardin, Terry. 2015. "Rationality in politics and its limits," *Global Discourse* 5(2), 177–190.

Noh, Yuree, Sharan Grewal, and M. Tahir Kilavuz. 2024. "Regime support and gender quotas in autocracies," *American Political Science Review* 118(2), 706–723.

Nye, Joseph S. Jr. 1990. "Soft power," *Foreign Policy* 80, 153–171.

Ozturk, Ahmet Erdi. 2021. "Islam and foreign policy: Turkey's ambivalent religious soft power in the authoritarian turn," *Religions* 12(1), 1–16.

Paris, Roland. 2019. "Can middle powers save the liberal world order," Chatham House Briefing, June 18, www.chathamhouse.org/2019/06/can-middle-powers-save-liberal-world-order.

Paris, Roland. 2020. "The right to dominate: How old ideas about sovereignty pose new challenges for world order," *International Organization* 74(3), 453–489.

Pattison, James. 2021. "The international responsibility to protect in a post-liberal order," *International Studies Quarterly* 65(4), 891–904.

Pevehouse, Jon C. 2005. *Democracy from above*, Cambridge, Cambridge University Press.

Piccioli, Matteo. 2024. "Human rights deteriorated globally in 2024, watchdog reports," JURISTnews, November 22, www.jurist.org/news/2024/11/global-rights-project-report-fails-more-than-half-the-worlds-countries/.

Piccone, Ted. 2018. "China's long game on human rights at the United Nations," Brookings, Research, www.brookings.edu/articles/chinas-long-game-on-human-rights-at-the-united-nations/.

Putnam, Robert D. 1988. "Diplomacy and domestic politics: The logic of two-level games," *International Organization* 42(2), 427–460.

Raymond, Mark, and Justin Sherman. 2024. "Authoritarian multilateralism in the global cyber regime complex: The double transformation of an international diplomatic practice," *Contemporary Security Policy* 45(1), 110–140.

Richter, Thomas. 2020. "New petro-aggression in the Middle East: Saudi Arabia in the spotlight," *Global Policy* 11(1), 93–102.

Rossiter, Ash, and Brendon J. Cannon. 2022. "Turkey's rise as a drone power: trial by fire," *Defense and Security Analysis* 38(2), 210–229.

Ruggie, John Gerard. 1992. "Multilateralism: The anatomy of an institution," *International Organization* 46(3), 561–598.

Sabatini, Christopher. 2014. "Meaningless multilateralism: In international diplomacy, South America chooses quantity over quality," Foreign Affairs, August 8, www.foreignaffairs.com/articles/south-america/2014-08-08/meaningless-multilateralism.

Sakr, Naomi. 2016. "Media 'globalisation' as a survival strategy for authoritarian regimes in the Arab Middle East," in Terry Flew, Petros Iosifidis and Jeanette Steemers, eds., *Global Media and National Policies*, New York, Palgrave Macmillan, 173–189.

Sandal, Nukhet A. 2014. "Middle powerhood as a legitimation strategy in the developing world: The cases of Brazil and Turkey," *International Politics* 51, 693–708.

Schatz, Edward. 2009. "The soft authoritarian tool kit: Agenda-setting power in Kazakhstan and Kyrgyzstan," *Comparative Politics* 41(2), 203–222.

Seven, Ümit. 2024. "Mediation as a state enterprise in Türkiye," CSS-ETH Zürich, September, https://css.ethz.ch/content/dam/ethz/special-interest/gess/cis/center-for-securities-studies/pdfs/CSSAnalyse346-EN.pdf.

Siccardi, Francesco. 2021. "How Syria changed Turkey's foreign policy," Carnegie Europe, September 14, https://carnegieendowment.org/research/2021/09/how-syria-changed-turkeys-foreign-policy?lang=en¢er=europe.

Siniver, Asaf, and Gerasimos Tsourapas. 2023. "Middle powers and soft-power rivalry: Egyptian-Israeli competition in Africa," *Foreign Policy Analysis* 19(2), advance online.

SIPRI. 2019. "Military spending and arms import by Iran, Saudi Arabia, Qatar, and the UAE," May, www.sipri.org/sites/default/files/2019-05/fs_1905_gulf_milex_and_arms_transfers.pdf.

Soyaltin-Colella, Digdem, and Tolga Demiryol. 2023. "Unusual middle power activism and regime survival: Turkey's drone warfare and its regime-boosting effects," *Third World Quarterly* 44(4), 724–743.

Svolik, Milan. 2012. *The Politics of Authoritarian Rule*, Cambridge, Cambridge University Press.

Tepeciklioğlu, Elem Eyrice, Francois Vreÿ, and Bahar Baser. 2023. "Introduction Turkey and Africa: Motivations, challenges and future prospects," *Journal of Balkan and Near Eastern Studies* 26, 289–294.

tho Seeth, Amanda. 2023. "Indonesia's Islamic peace diplomacy: Crafting a role model for moderate Islam," GIGA Focus Asia, 2, www.giga-hamburg.de/en/publications/giga-focus/indonesia-s-islamic-peace-diplomacy-crafting-role-model-for-moderate-islam.

Townshend, Estelle Jane. 2020. "Religion and political survival: The regional strategies of Iran, Saudi Arabia, the UAE and Qatar," PhD Thesis. The University of Waikato.

Transparency International. 2019. "Corruption as statecraft: Using corrupt practices as foreign policy tools," https://ti-defence.org/wp-content/uploads/2019/11/DSPCorruptionasStatecraft251119.pdf.

Turhan, Yunus. 2023. "Turkish humanitarian assistance during the COVID-19 pandemic: Focus on Africa," *Journal of Balkan and Near Eastern Studies* 26, 327–345.

Tuyloglu, Y. 2021. Turkish Development Assistance as a Foreign Policy Tool and Its Discordant Locations. German Institute for International and Security Affairs (Stiftung Wissenschaft und Politik).

Uniacke, Robert. 2021. "Authoritarianism in the information age: State branding, depoliticizing and 'de-civilizing' of online civil society in Saudi Arabia and the United Arab Emirates," *British Journal of Middle Eastern Studies* 48(5), 979–999.

V-Dem. 2024. "Democracy winning and losing at the ballot," Gothenburg, V-Dem Institute, https://v-dem.net/documents/44/v-demdr2024highres.pdf.

Verhoeven, Harry. 2018. "The gulf and the horn: Changing geographies of security interdependence and competing visions of regional order," *Civil Wars* 20(3), 333–357.

Von Soest, Christian, and Julia Grauvogel. 2017. "Identity, procedures and performance: How authoritarian regimes legitimize their rule," *Contemporary Politics* 23(3), 287–305.

Waddell, Benjamin. 2018. "Venezuela oil fueled the rise and fall of Nicaragua's Ortega regime," The Conversation, August 21, https://theconversation.com/venezuelan-oil-fueled-the-rise-and-fall-of-nicaraguas-ortega-regime-100507.

Waldmeier, Lena Moral. 2017. "Prestige aid: The case of Saudi Arabia and Malaysia," Durham Global Security Institute, DGSi Working Paper no. 3.

Walsh, Joe. 2020. "U.S. military: Iran is sending arms and troops to help Venezuela," Forbes, December 2, www.forbes.com/sites/joewalsh/2020/12/02/us-military-iran-is-sending-arms-and-troops-to-help-venezuela/?sh=3fcee85a4a31.

Wendt, Alexander. 1999. *Social Theory of International Relations*, Cambridge, Cambridge University Press.

Wezeman, Pieter D., Katarina Djokic, Mathew George, Zain Hussain and Siemon T. Wezeman. 2024. "Trends in international arms transfers, 2023," SIPRI Fact Sheet, March, www.sipri.org/sites/default/files/2024-03/fs2403at2023.pdf.

Wohlforth, William C., Benjamin de Carvalho, Halvard Leira, and Iver B. Neuman. 2018. "Moral authority and status in international relations: Good states and the social dimensions of status seeking," *Review of International Studies* 44(3), 526–546.

Wüst, A., & Nicolai, K. (2022). Cultural diplomacy and the reconfiguration of soft power: Evidence from Morocco. Mediterranean Politics, 28(4), 554–579.

Yarhi-Milo, Keren. 2023. "Why smart leaders do stupid things: Is foreign policy rational," Foreign Affairs, November/December.

Zeineddine, Cornelia. 2017. "Employing nation branding in the Middle East – United Arab Emirates (UAE) and Qatar," *Management & Marketing: Challenges for the Knowledge Society* 12(2), 208–221.

Zumbrägel, Tobias, and Thomas Demmelhuber. 2020. "Temptations of autocracy: How Saudi Arabia influences and attracts its neighbourhood," *Journal of Arabian Studies* 10(1), 51–71.

Cambridge Elements

International Relations

Series Editors

Jon C. W. Pevehouse
University of Wisconsin–Madison

Jon C. W. Pevehouse is the Mary Herman Rubinstein Professor of Political Science and Public Policy at the University of Wisconsin–Madison. He has published numerous books and articles in IR in the fields of international political economy, international organizations, foreign policy analysis, and political methodology. He is a former editor of the leading IR field journal, International Organization.

Tanja A. Börzel
Freie Universität Berlin

Tanja A. Börzel is the Professor of political science and holds the Chair for European Integration at the Otto-Suhr-Institute for Political Science, Freie Universität Berlin. She holds a PhD from the European University Institute, Florence, Italy. She is coordinator of the Research College "The Transformative Power of Europe," as well as the FP7-Collaborative Project "Maximizing the Enlargement Capacity of the European Union" and the H2020 Collaborative Project "The EU and Eastern Partnership Countries: An Inside-Out Analysis and Strategic Assessment." She directs the Jean Monnet Center of Excellence "Europe and its Citizens."

Edward D. Mansfield
University of Pennsylvania

Edward D. Mansfield is the Hum Rosen Professor of Political Science, University of Pennsylvania. He has published well over 100 books and articles in the area of international political economy, international security, and international organizations. He is Director of the Christopher H. Browne Center for International Politics at the University of Pennsylvania and former program co-chair of the American Political Science Association.

Editorial Team

International Relations Theory
Jeffrey T. Checkel, European University Institute, Florence

International Security
Jon C. W. Pevehouse, University of Wisconsin–Madison

International Political Economy
Edward D. Mansfield, University of Pennsylvania
Stefanie Walter, University of Zurich

International Organisations
Tanja A. Börzel, Freie Universität Berlin

About the Series

The Cambridge Elements Series in International Relations publishes original research on key topics in the field. The series includes manuscripts addressing international security, international political economy, international organizations, and international relations.

Cambridge Elements

International Relations

Elements in the Series

After Hedging: Hard Choices for the Indo-Pacific States between the US and China
Kai He and Huiyun Feng

IMF Lending: Partisanship, Punishment, and Protest
M. Rodwan Abouharb and Bernhard Reinsberg

Building Pathways to Peace: State–Society Relations and Security Sector Reform
Nadine Ansorg and Sabine Kurtenbach

Drones, Force and Law: European Perspectives
David Hastings Dunn and Nicholas J. Wheeler With Jack Davies, Zeenat Sabur

The Selection and Tenure of Foreign Ministers Around the World
Hanna Bäck, Alejandro Quiroz Flores and Jan Teorell

Lockean Liberalism in International Relations
Alexandru V. Grigorescu and Claudio J. Katz

Tip-toeing through the Tulips with Congress: How Congressional Attention Constrains Covert Action
Dani Kaufmann Nedal and Madison V. Schramm

Social Cues: How the Liberal Community Legitimizes Humanitarian War
Jonathan A. Chu

Environmental Ethics of War
Tamar Meisels

When Hedging Fails: Structural Uncertainty, Protective Options, and Geopolitical (Im)Prudence in Smaller Powers' Behaviour
Alexander Korolev

Norms, Practices, and Social Change in Global Politics
Steven Bernstein, Aarie Glas and Marion Laurence

The Rise of Authoritarian Middle-Powers and What It Means for World Politics
Marie-Eve Desrosiers and Nic Cheeseman

A full series listing is available at www.cambridge.org/EIR

For EU product safety concerns, contact us at Calle de José Abascal, 56–1°,
28003 Madrid, Spain or eugpsr@cambridge.org.

www.ingramcontent.com/pod-product-compliance
Ingram Content Group UK Ltd.
Pitfield, Milton Keynes, MK11 3LW, UK
UKHW021959030326
468620UK00021B/814